Fascism

Key Concepts in Political Theory

Charles Jones and Richard Vernon, *Patriotism*
Roger Griffin, *Fascism*

Fascism

An Introduction to Comparative Fascist Studies

Roger Griffin

polity

The right of Roger Griffin to be identified as Author of this Work has been asserted in accordance with the UK Copyright, Designs and Patents Act 1988.

First published in 2018 by Polity Press
Reprinted in 2018, 2019, 2020 (twice), 2021, 2022 (twice)

Polity Press
65 Bridge Street
Cambridge CB2 1UR, UK

Polity Press
101 Station Landing
Suite 300
Medford, MA 02155, USA

ISBN-13: 978-1-5095-2067-1
ISBN-13: 978-1-5095-2068-8 (pb)

A catalogue record for this book is available from the British Library.

Library of Congress Cataloging-in-Publication Data

Names: Griffin, Roger, 1948- author.
Title: Fascism / Roger Griffin.
Description: Medford, Massachusetts : Polity Press, 2018. | Series: Key Concepts in Political Theory | Includes bibliographical references and index.
Identifiers: LCCN 2017040401 (print) | LCCN 2017047571 (ebook) | ISBN 9781509520718 (Epub) | ISBN 9781509520671 (Hardback) | ISBN 9781509520688 (Paperback)
Subjects: LCSH: Fascism.
Classification: LCC JC481 (ebook) | LCC JC481 .G694 2018 (print) | DDC 320.53/3--dc23
LC record available at https://lccn.loc.gov/2017040401

Typeset in 10.5 on 12 pt Sabon
by Fakenham Prepress Solutions, Fakenham, Norfolk NR21 8NN
Printed and bound in Great Britain by CPI Group (UK) Ltd, Croydon

For further information on Polity, visit our website:
politybooks.com

Contents

Acknowledgements

This brief, but hopefully substantial, introduction to fascist studies owes an obvious debt to a small group of academics, speaking a wide variety of mother tongues, who pioneered the application of methodological empathy to understanding the nature of fascism. Their works became available between the 1960s and when I started my own research into fascism in 1985 and convinced me that the premises on which I was working were not totally aberrant (despite the enduring scepticism of some eminent historians). It is also indebted to a larger number of colleagues who approached fascist studies in a way either influenced by or convergent with my theory of 'palingenetic ultranationalism' in a critical but collaborative and generous-hearted spirit. The resulting synergies enabled genuine and rapid progress to be made away from a sustained period dominated by a curious methodological naivety and numerous idiosyncratic theories of fascism of minimal value to practising historians and political scientists.

It is a happy coincidence that the publication of this guide to fascism as a political theory coincides with the formation of the International Association for Comparative Fascist Studies (COMFAS) at the Central European University in Budapest, a fitting symbol of the way what used to be little more than a loose collection of arbitrary, almost amateur guesses about how to write about fascism has grown into a dynamic and cohesive sub-discipline. All those academics cited approvingly in this volume are implicitly acknowledged here, but several helped considerably to improve the first draft, notably my editor at Polity, George Owers (who showed remarkable patience as the project became more protracted and had a decisive impact on the final shape that it took), and my fellow adventurers in research into fascism and neo-fascism, Aristotle Kallis, Paul Jackson, Anton Shekhovtsov, David Roberts and Jakub Drabik.

What sparked my interest in fascism was the synchronicity of Mariella Demartini coming into my life and, with her, a magic portal through which to enter Italian culture, history, and language, just at a time when I was teaching a course on 'theories of fascism' with my head of department, Dr Robert Murray, at what was destined to become Oxford Brookes University. He had survived as a soldier fighting with the Anglo-American forces in Italy to defeat fascism, and he now wanted to understand as an academic just what it was he had been fighting and fighting for. It is to Mariella and Robert that this book is dedicated.

Campomorone and Oxford, August 2017

1

Introduction: Why Fascism is a 'Key Concept'

What then is fascism?

Some sixteen centuries ago, St Augustine of Hippo wrote in Book XI of his *Confessions*: 'What then is time? If no one asks me, I know what it is. If I wish to explain it to him who asks, I do not know.' A similar problem is posed by fascism. Most people who have been educated in the West instinctively 'know what fascism is' until they have to explain it to someone else, at which point the attempted definition tends to get increasingly convoluted and incoherent (an assertion that could be tested as a seminar exercise!). The rationale for the addition of this title to Polity's 'Key Concepts in Political Theory' series is that not only is it impossible simply to state 'what fascism is' but, a century after the word came into being to refer to a new Italian political movement and programme, its definition as a term of political and historical analysis is still bewilderingly varied and hotly debated. Hence the need for this 'beginner's guide', conceived for those studying at any level in the historical or political sciences who have reached the point where they have been recommended (or, even better, spontaneously feel the need for) a synoptic account of fascist studies, a relatively compact and accessible definition of fascism, and a brief overview of its main features, history and evolution when this definition is applied to actual policies, movements and events.

Study guides in the humanities run the risk of being frustratingly abstract and opaque, reminiscent of an instruction manual for assembling a flat-pack table tennis table which makes sense only once the table has been assembled, leaving some mysterious nuts, bolts and washers left over (I speak from experience). Nevertheless, I hope that what follows will demonstrate that, while fascism may be a frustratingly elusive topic when it comes to identifying the definitional features that distinguish it from other forms of far-right movements and regimes, perhaps for that very reason it can also be a highly absorbing and fulfilling one to study. In the first place, fascism supplies an outstanding example of the sound academic principle that, at an advanced level, no one can study or write the history of any aspect of a major topic in the human sciences effectively without first clarifying its conceptual contours and establishing a 'working definition' with due regard to how the discipline has approached it in the past. Second, if the core argument of this volume is accepted, a fascinating narrative emerges of how fascism, since its inauspicious beginnings in March 1919 as a new but insignificant political force launched by a motley assembly of Italian war veterans, grew in the interwar period into a devastating 'world-historical' force and continues to impact on contemporary history in a number of ways, despite the radical decline in its support base and potency since 1945. Finally, even if you disagree with the thesis put forward here, it should at least help you to locate where you stand in the ongoing debate about fascism, to formulate what you find unconvincing in what has become the dominant 'school of thought' within comparative fascist studies, and to present your own take on fascism more confidently within the context of an essay project or formal programme of studies.

Why fascism is not like a duck

Yet the way 'fascism' is bandied about so liberally and assertively in public discourse could suggest that dedicating a whole volume (even a thin one like this) just to clarifying its connotations and surveying the type of historical phenomena it embraces is somewhat 'over the top'. For many journalists and political commentators, it is clearly self-evident what fascism means. At the height of the US presidential campaign of 2016, for example, Republican candidate Gary Johnson, when asked if Donald Trump was a fascist, replied cryptically: 'It walks like a duck, quacks like a duck.' Leaving aside the allusion to the cartoon character Donald Duck, this reply implied that it could be directly deduced from Trump's political pronouncements and behaviour that he was indeed 'a duck', in this case a fascist (Pager 2016). But, as should become obvious after a moment's reflection, at least to readers of this book if not to presidential candidates or their interviewers, the entity 'fascism' cannot be compared to a waterfowl. A duck is an objective, living animal that can be defined biologically in terms of its empirically established family or genus (*Anatidae*) in the animal kingdom and comprises several objectively identifiable variants (species). 'Duck' is thus a *taxonomic* concept within the natural sciences about whose application to phenomena in the real world there exists an expert consensus, at least within the professional discipline of zoology – though it is worth noting that even the duck family is prone to be confused by untrained eyes with several types of water bird from other branches of evolution that look similar, such as loons, coots, divers, grebes and gallinules.

By contrast, those concerned with the philosophy of the human sciences have shown conclusively that there can be no equivalent consensus about the definition of 'fascism' – or of any other generic concept used in making sense of politics, society or history.[1] It follows that the meaning of fascism, as of every generic 'key concept' in history, social, or political science, is bound to be a subject of debate and disagreement, and any scholarly consensus about its meaning is inevitably both partial (as more research illuminates new facts, relationships and issues and identifies new topics, patterns and interconnections) and ephemeral (as both history and the historiography move on). This is why fascist studies will always be 'work in progress', and the key generic concept that lies at their heart will continue to be contested as long as academics consider its characterization a worthy object of intellectual effort.

The narrative history of 'fascism' that emerges

It may help prepare the reader for what follows to outline the particular historical narrative that emerges in this volume on the basis of how fascism is being conceptualized here. The first thing to note is that the book will follow standard practice by restricting upper-case 'Fascism' to Mussolini's movement and regime and using lower-case 'fascism' for the vast family of movements and associated phenomena to which it gave rise in many other countries, and which is known collectively as 'generic fascism'. It is generic fascism as a key concept in politics that is the subject here. Once its most commonly used scholarly definition (to be established in chapter 3) is applied, fascism can be seen as playing a central role in shaping a number of momentous events that occurred in the early twentieth century as a direct or indirect result of the alliance of Fascist Italy and Nazi Germany: the war they jointly fought as founders of the 'Berlin–Rome Axis' against many Western democracies between 1939 and 1945; the alliance of the Third Reich and the Soviet Union from 1939 to 1941, when Central and Eastern Europe were divided into two 'spheres of influence' in accordance with the Molotov–Ribbentrop Pact; and the persecution, forced migration, enslavement, starvation, and systematic mass murder of countless millions of civilians which ensued when the Third Reich unilaterally terminated the pact on 22 June 1941 with a large-scale attack on Russian positions in Poland.

After the Nazi invasion of Russia and the Japanese attack on Pearl Harbor in December 1941, which brought the United States into the war, the European conflict triggered by the rise of fascism, and consolidated by collaboration with home-grown fascist support in Nazi-occupied countries and pro-fascist governments elsewhere, quickly escalated into a truly global one, with major theatres of operations in Europe and in Asia, on land, on oceans and in the skies. No wonder some historians have seen fascism, along with communism, as the dominant factor in shaping history from 1918 to 1945 to the point that they talk of a 'fascist era' or of fascism as 'an epochal movement'. There is some sense in this, since, even if only three fully fledged fascist regimes were established – those in Italy under Benito Mussolini, in Germany under Adolf Hitler and in Croatia under Ante Pavelić, and only the first two in peacetime – numerous movements trying to emulate them sprang up in Europeanized countries, some serving as puppet governments and thus proving vital to Nazism's success in maintaining control of the 'New European Order' for as long as it did. In addition, a number of dictatorships 'fascistized' themselves in Europe and Latin America as a mark of fascism's apparent hegemony and its prospects of ultimate victory in the modern political age.

After 1945, the political space for fascism was drastically reduced, and the concept itself can be argued to have long since lost its 'key' status in the contemporary political world. But we shall see that, when an ideological definition of fascism, rather than one that stresses its interwar manifestation as a uniformed paramilitary movement or totalitarian state, is applied to post-1945 history, it highlights the existence at any one time of many hundreds of formations and activities (whether in the form of parties, movements, groupuscules, websites or fanatical loners) dedicated to the core ideals of their 'classic' interwar models, albeit significantly revised and updated so as to combat the new enemies of their ultimate cause. Moreover, the persistence of fascist fanaticism about awakening slumbering forces of extreme nationalism and racism, even in just one isolated individual, poses a continuing risk of causing sporadic but potentially devastating terrorist attacks on civil society. This suggests that many thousands of disoriented individuals who feel unable to tolerate what they see as the cultural chaos or 'decadence' of the modern world persist in seeing the defeat of the Axis powers as a historical catastrophe. Undaunted, they still long to play a part in inaugurating a new fascist era, or at least in keeping fascist ideals alive, by exploiting any situation or technology which allows them to transmit the urgency of the need for national or racial rebirth based on their ideals of a more homogeneous, more heroic, more epic civilization.

More reasons to dedicate a volume to fascism as a 'Key Concept in Political Theory'

'Fascism' deserves to be included in Polity's series not just for its decisive impact on the course of interwar history or because, even if the fascist utopia lives out a subsistence existence in marginalized political counter-cultures all over the Westernized world, it can still inspire acts of extreme violence. It is also important for the term to be used precisely and forensically wherever possible because of two widespread misuses, or abuses, of it as a concept that have seeped into public discourse and into the language of the media, compromising its precision and analytical value. On the one hand, it has been widely reduced to a colloquialism for any political system, state policy or example of social mores that is held to limit personal freedom, individual choice and self-expression in a manipulative or authoritarian spirit. The campaign to raise awareness of global warming, the state-sponsored fluoridation of water, the machinations of big business, the bureaucracy of the European Union, government attempts to encourage the public to stop smoking, political correctness, the damage that the fashion industry does to self-image and healthy eating habits, even the state taxation system – all have been tarred with the brush of fascism. Nor is this dilution of the term's meaning unique to the West. In 2002 the Muslim creationist Adnan Oktar, also known as Harun Yahya (2002), published *Fascism: The Bloody Ideology of Darwinism*.

A second area in which the term is subject to distortion is in political commentary, debate and protest. To call opponents 'fascist' instantly delegitimizes and demonizes them in the eyes of their critics, whether they are the Republican Tea Party, President Obama, Donald Trump, Vladimir Putin, Saddam Hussein, Bashar al-Assad, the state of Israel, the US federal state, the Brussels Eurocracy, or any anti-socialist dictatorship, anti-populist or excessively populist force. After 9/11, it became common for political Islam (Islamism, or, more precisely, global Salafi jihad) to be referred to as 'Islamofascism', a use sanctioned by George W. Bush. More recently, during the Russian–Ukrainian conflict, both sides called each other fascists. Meanwhile, some journalists writing for the 'quality press' assure us that China has mutated from a communist into a fascist state (e.g. Becker 2002). The most serious effect of such a sloppy use of the term 'fascism', whatever its cathartic effect as a pejorative or expletive term, is that it has contributed to the profound confusion that prevails about how to describe the advocates of particular right-wing forms of democratic politics who attack multiculturalism, the free movement of labour, the Islamization of society, big government, and international bodies such as the EU and the UN, but do so *democratically*, from within the institutions of representative government that they have no intention of dismantling. The prevailing term for this increasingly important current in contemporary politics, 'populism', raises problematic issues of its own, not least because it is frequently conflated with 'fascism', and it will be necessary to return to it in chapter 5.

Because of these two main areas in which the analytical, heuristic value of 'fascism' has been eroded and degraded through lack of precision, considerable space will have to be devoted in this volume to establishing the conceptual framework which will be used to outline its pre- and postwar history. However, as we have indicated, this can take place only after the 'pre-history' of contemporary attempts to refine its definition and establish its connotations and significance as a concept has been sketched.

The structure of this book

The structure of the book emerges naturally from this agenda. Chapter 2 looks at the rich history of Marxist interpretations of fascism, the first of which were published two years before Mussolini actually became *duce*, and also provides a sample of the deep confusion that prevailed for decades in fascist studies outside Marxism on definitional issues. The result of this acute lack of consensus was a proliferation of idiosyncratic theories of the term which found minimal resonance or practical application among either historians or political scientists.

Chapter 3 then proposes a particular model, or what Max Weber termed 'ideal type',[2] of generic fascism, whose adoption by a growing number of researchers all over the world since the 1990s has resulted for the first time in a constant flow of impressive articles, monographs and collections of essays on aspects of generic fascism or particular movements with a high level of internal coherence and complementarity within the field. These two chapters thus offer a sort of 'narrative history' of the long, and eventually successful, struggle to provide 'fascism' with conceptual and definitional coherence. It has been deliberately organized and shaped to prepare the reader for the particular connotations and applications the term acquires in the book. (It goes without saying that any other expert would have given the term contrasting conceptual contours reflecting his or her own interpretation, in some cases producing a radically different volume in the series.)

Chapter 4 then applies the theoretical approach that has just been established to the interwar period by providing many examples of the way particular fascist phenomena always combine common ideological elements identified by the generic model with highly diverse and idiosyncratic features, a synthesis which gives each individual manifestation of generic fascism its unique texture and 'personality' within the historical process.

Following this, chapter 5 offers a synoptic overview of the evolution of postwar and contemporary fascism to illustrate the sheer variety of the species that can be seen as perpetuating the genus to this day (that is, if the 'working definition' proposed in this volume is accepted). The chapter hopes to convince the reader that, even though the 'era of fascism' died symbolically with the shooting of Mussolini by partisans near the shore of Lake Como and with Hitler's suicide in his Berlin bunker in April 1945, the dreams they held of an ultra-nationalist new order endure on an international scale that they could never have imagined, though often with forms, modes of transmission, contents, tactics and utopian goals which would be barely recognizable to either of them.

The book ends with a postscript (chapter 6) which suggests the key principles of comparative fascist studies to be taken away by students for their own work. It then recommends how even those new to this specialist area might be able to make a substantive contribution to its further progress through the deliberate choice of topics and research questions which are informed by the latest trends and issues evident from recent publications, to which this slim volume can only allude. If they choose to do so, they would be joining an academic community engaged in a sub-discipline which, after a long period of adolescence, seems finally to be entering a dynamic stage of productive maturity and truly international productivity. Long gone are the days when one of the most eminent anglophone experts on Italian Fascism of the time reacted to my sheepish confession that I was writing a doctoral thesis on fascist ideology with the encouraging words: 'My boy, there is no such thing. Have another glass of sherry'.

2
Making Sense of Fascism: Marxist and Early Liberal Approaches

The quest for a definition

The attempt to arrive at a satisfactory definition of fascism has been likened to the mystical quest for the Holy Grail (Blinkhorn 2000: 5), to the prospector's devotion to 'unearthing a final pure lode' of lexical gold (Bosworth 2009: 5) and, even more dispiritingly, to 'searching for a black cat in a dark and possibly empty room' (Whittam 1995: 1). This chapter surveys one of the two main routes now followed by the intrepid trekkers who, undeterred by such doubting Thomases, have embarked on this expedition ever since, in March 1919, Mussolini founded the first of a planned network of Fasci italiani di combattimento (Italian Combat Leagues) in Italy's most dynamic city, Milan, to keep the spirit of the trenches alive.

The Fascist programme, announced to a small audience gathered in a meeting room of the Industrial Alliance headquarters in Piazza San Sepolcro, made it clear that the fledgling movement's mission was to give rise to a militant vanguard dedicated to the total transformation of Italy in the spirit of *combattentismo*, the extreme, self-sacrificial patriotism of veterans, especially the army's elite assault troops, the Arditi, who had survived the horrific conditions of trench warfare in the mountains long enough to witness the Entente victory. Within weeks the new force in Italian politics was being called 'Fascism' – the connotations of the Roman symbol of state authority, the *Fasces*, came later – and by 1922 a new generic term, 'fascism', entered the political lexicon.

The first route, towards making sense of this new concept, which can be traced back to the earliest days of Fascism, is made up of Marxist approaches, all of which, though they can be extremely nuanced and original in detail, assume fascism to be inextricably related to the anti-socialist reaction of the bourgeoisie, financial elites, big business and global capitalism. Such links are so axiomatic for the revolutionary left that Max Horkheimer, a leading member of the Frankfurt School of Marxism, famously warned in his essay 'The Jews and Europe', published in *Zeitschrift für Sozialforschung* in 1939, that 'Whoever is not prepared to talk about capitalism should also remain silent about fascism' (quoted in Kellner 1989: 67).

In addition, this chapter will consider briefly another category of responses to the problem of defining fascism, one which is far too disparate and unproductive to be thought of as a 'tradition' or a 'school': that of academic 'liberals' (a generic term for a very broad church of non-Marxist researchers and professional academics) who, for almost seven decades, offered highly idiosyncratic and often incoherent interpretations and paradigms which defy neat classification under various subheadings (for a sustained attempt at categorization, see Hagtvet and Kühnl 1980). Not surprisingly, these proved of limited value for meeting the pragmatic interpretive and definitional needs of practising historians and political scientists who were researching extreme right-wing phenomena in the modern age.

The Marxist school: Fascism as the vanguard of capitalist reaction

We have seen that, unlike most political concepts, the origins of the term 'fascism' can be traced symbolically to a particular time and place, namely 23 March 1919 in

Milan. It is worth noting that the new *Fasci* formed a direct successor of the League of Revolutionary Action (Fascio d'Azione Rivoluzionaria), which Mussolini had set up in 1914 as a pressure group to help whip up popular support for Italy's involvement in the First World War on the side of the Triple Entente. Its members went on to play a prominent role in the 'interventionist' movement, where they were soon being referred to as '*Fascisti*'. From the outset, then, 'Fascist' had dynamic, modernizing, revolutionary connotations for its supporters, not reactionary or conservative ones.

Initially, though, 'fascism' referred specifically to Mussolini's new movement, and it was left-wing Italian intellectuals, convinced of its repressive and reactionary nature as a violent assault on the working-class movement, who made the first attempt to interpret it as a more substantive and general political phenomenon. The context of their concern to understand its nature as a new factor in Italy's, and possibly modern, political life was revolutionary socialism's defeat in the *biennio rosso* (1919–20), the 'red two years' when tensions between the revolutionary left and militant nationalists reached boiling point in parts of Central and Northern Italy. The resulting conflict with the local *Fasci* that had sprung up to defeat 'Bolshevism' and militant socialism occurred against the background of profound economic, political and social chaos that afflicted several parts of the country, especially in rural areas, following the end of the war. In 1922, the Italian reformist socialist Giovanni Zibordi published his *Critica socialista del fascismo*, which initially identified three radical components at work in the Fascist assault on the left: a counter-revolution of the 'big' or *haute* bourgeoisie against the 'red' revolution; a revolution by the middle classes against the liberal regime; and a (para)military revolution against the state. But Zibordi's conclusion shed such nuances when he went on to define fascism reductively as 'a socio-political movement of the big bourgeoisie, or at least a movement that it has successfully used and exploited' (Beetham 1983: 88–96).

This class analysis set the tone for the vast outpouring of socialist, and especially Marxist, analyses of fascism that continue to this day, all of which assume the axiomatically *capitalist* nature of fascism, whether (at the very most) counter-revolutionary and partially autonomous or (at the very least) arch-reactionary and controlled by the bourgeoisie. It also presciently expressed uncertainty about whether the capitalist classes directly created fascism as a weapon against revolutionary socialism (the 'agent' theory) or appropriated it to this end after it had come into being independently (the 'Bonapartist' theory). Rather than modify their dualistic theory (inherited from the writings of Marx and Engels) of socialism's revolutionary war against a single antagonist or arch-enemy, capitalism, Marxists have generally denied that in the interwar period they were suddenly faced by a rival revolutionary and, at bottom, *anti-capitalist, anti-bourgeois* force (see Pellicani 2012) which pursued an alternative totalizing vision to Bolshevism, namely that of a new form of modern society based not on radical socialism but on radical nationalism.

Given the confidence of Zibordi's prediction of the ephemeral nature of fascism, Mussolini's successful bid for state power in 'the March on Rome' of October 1922 threw European communists and radical socialists of many persuasions into disarray over the significance of the unexpected turn of events. This was reflected in the Fourth Congress of the Soviet-dominated Communist International (the 'Comintern'), which was held in Petrograd and Moscow in November and December 1922, just as the future *duce* began his premiership. Grigory Zinoviev's reaction was incoherent, dismissing Fascism as 'a farce' that would soon be consigned to history yet, at the same time, anticipating similar events would take place in Central Europe. Amadeo Bordiga predicted that, now it had gained power to the extent that Mussolini was head of state, Fascism would be generally 'liberal and democratic', with the occasional violent episode. Antonio Gramsci was less sanguine, warning that Italy's Fascists, because of Mussolini's backing by the black-shirted squads (*squadristi*), had 'held in their hands the entire foundation of the state' even before taking office. Meanwhile, Karl Radek called Mussolini's appointment as prime minister 'the greatest defeat that socialism and communism have suffered' since 1917 (Riddell 2012: 106; see also Riddell 2014).

The agent theory

Despite the contradictory individual reactions, the foundation stones of the orthodox Soviet interpretation of generic fascism had been laid in the Final Resolution of the 1922 Congress. This concluded that its function was to act as capitalism's direct agent of class repression and the force through which the bourgeoisie conducted its offensive against the proletariat, its paramilitary soldiers serving as the 'White Guards' of counter-revolution. At the same time, it sought to gain a working-class following through the use of 'social demagogy'. But, armed with Marxism-Leninism, socialists could see clearly that 'the reckless promotion of fascist organization [was] the last card in the bourgeoisie's hand' and demonstrated that bourgeois rule was now 'possible only in the form of an undisguised dictatorship over the proletariat'. Certainly, this pseudo-revolutionary solution to liberal government's impotence to repress the rise of the working-class movement was likely to be resorted to elsewhere, and signs of the coming fascist threat were already visible in 'Czechoslovakia, Hungary, almost all the Balkan countries, Poland, Germany, Austria, America and even in countries like Norway'. However, in the long run, fascism's attempt to halt the progress of socialism was doomed (Fourth Congress of the Comintern 1922). By the time of the Fifth Comintern Congress in July 1924, six months before the inauguration of the *duce*'s regime, the 'agent theory' of fascism's nature had taken shape. It was declared 'the instrument of the big bourgeoisie for fighting the proletariat, when the legal means available to the state have proved insufficient to subdue them'. As such it represented 'the extra-legal arm of the big bourgeoisie for establishing and extending its dictatorship' (Beetham 1983: 152–3).

An important implication of the approach to fascism that crystallized in these two congresses was that the West's entire liberal democratic system devoted to maintaining capitalism, because of its bourgeois origins, was *de facto* in collusion with fascism, an assumption seemingly vindicated by the fact that Mussolini acted as 'democratic' head of a liberal parliamentary state between 1922 and 1925 before the seamless transition to becoming the radically nationalist and imperialist, and hence anti-Marxist and anti-proletarian, dictator of Fascist Italy. It is consistent with this premise not only that the conservative administrations which presided over Hitler's rise to power after the Wall Street Crash of 1929 were depicted by the Communist Party of Germany (KPD) as fascist, but that the social democrats of the SDP, rather than being treated as the natural allies of communists in the struggle against Nazism, were actually dismissed as fascist collaborators as well, or 'social fascists'. This position had already been anticipated in the Fifth Comintern Congress of 1924, where both Zinoviev and Trotsky agreed that 'Fascism and Social Democracy are two sides of the same instrument: capitalist dictatorship.' In the same vein, Stalin described them simply as 'twins' (Saba 1979: 196–7).

The equation of social democracy with fascism was to have particularly serious consequences in Germany, where it prevented any tactical alliance being formed between the KPD and SDP against Hitler, and even led in 1931 to a temporary collaboration of Nazis with communists to bring down the SDP in Prussia. It was only the Third Reich's brutal persecution of communists and the entire socialist movement after Hitler came to power that in 1935 belatedly brought about calls for a 'popular front', a rhetoric that was abruptly silenced once more with the announcement of the Nazi–Soviet 'Ribbentrop Pact' in 1939. Meanwhile, in Russia, Stalin persisted in using the term 'fascist' on occasion to discredit versions of Marxism-Leninism he rejected. Bitter conflicts between various left-wing factions, including social democrats and rival variants of Marxism, on the issue of fascism also had the effect of undermining the Spanish government's military campaign to defend the left-wing Republic during the Civil War against General Franco (identified as the embodiment of fascism by Marxist theory).

While judgements on social democracy's kinship with fascism vacillated, Comintern's official pronouncements on its reactionary nature were steadily shedding the more nuanced and pluralistic analyses of the early 1920s until a position emerged that reduced fascism to one of the chief manifestations of capitalism, denying it any autonomy in its relationship to the traditional state apparatus which served as the basis of capitalism's rule (or 'hegemony'). In 1931 Dmitri Manuilski's report on fascism to the Executive Committee of the Communist International (ECCI) declared that 'The fascist regime is not just any new type of state; it is one of the forms of bourgeois dictatorship characteristic of the imperialist epoch. Fascism grows organically out of bourgeois democracy' (Beetham 1983: 157–8). The idea that fascism was the agent of capitalism to the point of identity found its definitive formulation in the Bulgarian Georgi Dimitrov's seminal declaration at the Seventh Congress of Comintern in 1935 that 'Fascism is an open terrorist dictatorship of the most reactionary, the most chauvinistic, the most imperialistic elements of finance capital' (Dimitrov 1935).

Until the collapse of the USSR, the agent theory of fascism in its Dimitrovian formulation was the rigid dogma assumed in all textbooks and historical research throughout the Soviet Empire. This led to the remarkable situation where, for over four decades, the Iron Curtain between East and West Germany divided not just two entirely different ideological, political, economic and social systems but also two prolific yet utterly contrasting academic industries concerned with the analysis of Nazism and generic fascism. In the German Federal Republic, with the exception of some prominent left-wing historians who treated Nazism as a member of the far-flung family of fascism, mainstream scholarship was largely occupied with reconstructing the unique origins and course of the Third Reich, with minimal reference to the international fascism debate or parallels between the NSDAP and other movements or regimes – the right-wing historian Ernst Nolte, author of *Three Faces of Fascism* (1965), was a rare exception in this respect. Meanwhile, in the German Democratic Republic, Nazism was routinely treated as the most brutal and destructive manifestation of fascism, and hence as a latent potential of any capitalist system, with a deep kinship to all racist, expansionist or anti-communist movements and regimes, both interwar and after 1945, anywhere in the world.

In the past, such polarization has led to 'blind spots' on both sides, with many Marxist scholars unwilling to concede that Nazism could exert any serious attraction on segments of the urban or rural 'proletariat', while 'liberals' tended to neglect the importance of examining the real but complex collusion that some areas of German finance, big business and the commercial bourgeoisie developed with the Third Reich. This collusion was particularly conspicuous in such areas as the creation of the Reich's war economy, the build-up of its military-industrial complex, its ruthless suppression of the autonomy of socialism, communism and the labour movement in Germany and its European empire, its 'legal' expropriation of racial enemies, and its deployment of slave- and concentration-camp labour for its commercial and productive value.[1] But, outside the extensive 'Marxist camp' of scholarship, such phenomena are not taken to be evidence of the capitalist essence of fascism (Payne 1995: 443–5).

The Bonapartist thesis

We have seen that, as early as 1923, Zibordi suggested that fascism might be an autonomous political force 'used and exploited' by the bourgeoisie. This insight developed into a powerful alternative current within non-Comintern Marxist thinking generally, referred to as the 'Bonapartist' theory of fascism. In his essay 'The Eighteenth Brumaire of Louis Bonaparte' (1852), Marx had reflected on the failure of the socialist left to break through after the revolutionary events in Paris of 1848 and on Louis-Napoléon Bonaparte's rapid elevation from republican president to Emperor Napoléon III. In it he portrayed the reigns of both Napoleon I and Napoleon III as forms of autonomous military dictatorship which, however popular, crushed progressive working-class movements, and thereby were able to serve bourgeois interests while simultaneously retaining power over the bourgeoisie.

Used in the analysis of fascism, 'Bonapartism' provides an elegant way for Marxists to use a concept rooted in orthodox Marxist historical analysis to accommodate fascism within a scheme of history which denies it any genuine ideological novelty, populist base or revolutionary dynamic, thus leaving progress towards the ultimate realization of a socialist society in theory unimpeded by a 'new' ideological enemy. A characteristic feature of the term's application is that it encourages

Marxists to view any fascist regime (which for them extends to most anti-communist dictatorships and racist regimes) as an emergency or 'exceptional' state generated by the imperialist forces of capitalism (see Biver 2005). It is an ad hoc solution to a crisis that might suit elements within the bourgeoisie initially, and might whip up cross-class support with its populist and nationalist rhetoric, but proves inherently unstable and doomed to failure because of its internal class contradictions (Linton 1989: 109–16; Kitchen 1973).

Students new to this topic, and keen to appreciate the significant differences that can exist between the variants of the Bonapartist theory of fascism which recognizes its partial autonomy from capitalism, are urged to be aware of four thinkers in particular – August Thalheimer, Otto Bauer, Leon Trotsky and Antonio Gramsci – in the wider context of the Marxist anti-fascist struggle documented in Beetham (1983). Former Comintern thinker and activist Thalheimer, for example, argues in his 1930 essay 'On Fascism' (heavily influenced by his experience of the rise of Nazism) that, by using naked violence against not just the workers but also the bourgeois parliament, fascism represented a 'sudden leap' away both from Bonapartism and from earlier forms of state repression. Thus, far from being an agent of the bourgeoisie, fascism eventually turns out to be hostile to it (see Kitchen 1973). Otto Bauer, the Austrian social democrat who died in exile in Paris after the unsuccessful socialist uprising in 1934, not only recognized the relatively autonomous nature of Nazism from the bourgeoisie but saw it as the symptom of a wider civilizational crisis which would be resolved not by class struggle but by war (Linton 1989: 122–3).

Far less elaborated but more influential than the analyses of either Thalheimer or Bauer was Leon Trotsky's brief 1934 article 'Bonapartism and Fascism', which lambasted the 'Stalinist theory of fascism' as 'one of the most tragic examples of the injurious practical consequences that can follow from the substitution of the dialectical analysis of reality ... by abstract categories formulated upon the basis of a partial and insufficient historical experience' (Trotsky 1934). He is particularly caustic about the Comintern's habit of indiscriminately labelling any form of right-wing regime or movement 'fascist'.

Trotsky's own theory is shaped by the distinction he draws between two forms of Bonapartism. There is 'preventive Bonapartism', in which the bourgeoisie encourages the government to suspend the democratic process so as to ward off the danger of a fascist takeover, as in the presidential dictatorship that preceded Hitler (and presumably in Mussolini's parliamentary premiership before the creation of the Fascist state). Then there is 'Bonapartism of fascist origin' (similar to what Thalheimer calls 'fascism'), which occurs when reaction ceases to be a populist nationalist force and hardens into a militaristic state imposed on the whole of society, including the paramilitary forces of the bourgeoisie that brought it to power. Though he introduces important new nuances in the understanding of Bonapartism, he still shares Comintern's axiomatic assumption that both Bonapartism and fascism 'can only be the government of finance capital' and even asserts that Hitler's tasks are 'assigned him by monopoly capital' (Trotsky 1933). He also reflects the prevailing Marxist complacency about the eventual triumph of socialism in his assertion that 'all history shows that it is impossible to keep the proletariat enchained with the aid merely of the police apparatus' (Trotsky 1934).

Some of the most penetrating Marxist analyses of fascism before the Second World War were undertaken by the Italian communist Gramsci. The growing elaboration and sophistication of his analyses of how Fascism had come to power in 1925, when according to Comintern theory the objective material conditions instead pointed to a socialist victory, have been extensively explored by a number of scholars (e.g. Adamson 1980; Roberts 2011; Santoro 2012). These have shown in considerable detail how far he moved away from crudely deterministic theories of class conflict, dialectical materialism and socialist revolution, as well as documenting his growing recognition of the relative autonomy of ideology (the 'superstructure') from the socio-economic 'base' and the role played by spiritual and cultural crisis as drivers of historical reaction and change.

Two salient points of his extensive theoretical writings stand out in the context of this guide to fascism. First, in his last phase Gramsci portrayed the post-1918 period in Italy as full of possibilities for a (Marxist) revolution, but argued that Mussolini was able to exploit the societal crisis more effectively by announcing the imminent creation of a new powerful nationalist and ethical order and by deliberately fomenting 'Caesarism' – charismatic energies embodied in a leader. Unlike Bonapartism in late nineteenth-century France, Caesarism, as Gramsci saw it, could have a progressive, anti-reactionary dynamic – as Lenin had amply demonstrated (Santoro 2012: 277–86). Second, Gramsci analysed the crisis of 1929–33 in Germany which brought Hitler to power once again as one of left-revolutionary potential blocked by the power of superstructural forces – ideological factors such as the capitalist press, a reactionary civil society and educational system, conservative nationalism and institutional religion. These ensured that it was not a deeply divided left that triumphed but another Caesarist right-wing leader, Adolf Hitler, who persuasively offered the public the goal of realizing the reactionary, socially repressive utopia of a racial state to which he aspired by presenting it as a national revolution, a revolution of the entire *Volk* (Overy 2001).

All these Marxist theorists can be seen from a non-Marxist perspective as departing from the Comintern dogma on fascism in creative and significant ways, but also as remaining faithful to the axiom that socialism was the only progressive, emancipatory and revolutionary historical force at work after the First World War. As a consequence, they were unable to confront the possibility that fascism was driven by utopian ideals of a new order and an alternative modernity destined to supersede both liberalism and Marxism and which, *within its own terms*, could thus claim to be a rival revolution.

Later developments in Marxist theory

In the decades that have elapsed since Gramsci's death, these two main currents of Marxist interpretation of fascism have been perpetuated. The agent theory remained the official dogma of Comintern until its last congress in 1943 and, as we have seen, was then adopted mostly uncritically as the unchallenged axiom of all research carried out in Marxist regimes until the collapse of the Soviet Empire.[2] Meanwhile, the majority of the world's many socialist movements continue to invoke Trotsky's analysis of capitalism as the basis of their activism and revolutionary theory (Biver 2006), thereby ensuring that it is his variant of Bonapartism that is normally applied to the unfolding of capitalism's permanent crisis and continuous spawning of right-wing solutions. As a result, anti-communist military dictatorships (e.g. Pinochet's Chile) and populist forms of right-wing politics (e.g. Le Pen's Front National) have been routinely analysed in the left-wing press as fascist, however distant their relationship to Fascism or Nazism (e.g. Ira 2016). In the UK, for example, both the Anti-Nazi League, set up by the Socialist Worker's Party in 1977, and David Renton's *Fascism* (1999), which offers an important Marxist critique of recent non-Marxist analyses of fascism, are Trotskyist in inspiration.

However, it should be emphasized that, in the past, 'liberal', non-Marxist understanding of the Third Reich has been enriched by several extended analyses loosely based on idiosyncratic Bonapartist premises. The earliest was Franz Neumann's *Behemoth: The Structure and Practice of National Socialism 1933–1944* (1942), written while in exile in the US by an eminent member of the Frankfurt School of Marxism, which had taken refuge from the Third Reich in New York in 1935. In it, the principle of the autonomy of the fascist state is taken to its logical conclusion. Neumann portrays the regime as erecting the propagandistic façade of a powerful, efficient and homogeneous state, thus concealing its perpetual internal anarchy, as warring party officials, ministerial factions and ambitious leaders fought for power, united only by their commitment to military adventurism, personal ambition and the destruction of socialism. As a result, the traditional bourgeoisie remained impotent to control events.

A more conventional Bonapartist approach to fascism in power was adopted in the 1970s by the Franco-Greek Eurocommunist Nicos Poulantzas, who presented the Third Reich and Fascist Italy as 'exceptional capitalist states'. Drawing on Gramscian ideas of 'cultural hegemony', Poulantzas argued that they depended not just on bourgeois but also on populist support for their ideology and goals, reinforced by the extensive social engineering required in order to maintain them in power (Poulantzas 1979; see also Caplan 1977; Kershaw 1989: 63–5). Analysing the Third Reich as an 'exceptional state' dependent on extensive social control brings the study of fascism within the orbit of postwar non-Marxist theories of 'totalitarianism', especially the phenomenology of oppression explored by Hannah Arendt (1951). However, given the radical differences between Fascist and Nazi states in power, it is important to underline how misleading it is to see Nazism as the archetype, let alone the essence, of fascism, just as it is methodologically flawed to take Italian Fascism to be the template of all other fascisms (e.g. Wippermann 2009) – a point to which we will return.

It was in this period that Tim Mason, Britain's leading Marxist historian of Nazism, applied broadly Bonapartist assumptions to the detailed study of the fate of the working class and women under Nazism and to the analysis of the economic and political structure of the Third Reich and Fascist Italy. This led him to the conclusion, unthinkable for dogmatic Comintern 'agent theorists', that, far from directly serving the cause of capital, the 'primacy of politics' prevailed over narrow economic concerns. This meant 'that both the domestic and foreign policy of the National Socialist government became, from 1936 onward, increasingly independent of the influence of the economic ruling classes, and even in some essential aspects ran contrary to their collective interests' (Mason [1966] 1972: 175–7; see also Kershaw [1985] 2000: 49–50; Caplan 1995).

Following in Mason's footsteps, but also picking up themes from Thalheimer, the Hungarian Mihaly Vajda, in *Fascism as a Mass Movement*, argued that, though it is a 'capitalist form of rule', once in power fascism's commitment to expansionist war creates 'extraordinary political conditions and replaces normal bourgeois everyday life with a situation of constant tension, and the bourgeoisie finds this at least "uncomfortable"' (1976: 93). Vajda also set himself apart from mainstream Marxist analyses by highlighting fascism's dependency for coming to power on a mass movement regimented by paramilitary forces but seduced by the populist appeal of a 'totalistic' ideology. This ideology emphasized the 'uplifting of the nation', which he saw as the only recurring component of the very varied fascist movements that have arisen. Such an unusual concession by a Marxist suggests at least an affinity with the theory of fascism as a revolutionary movement of ultranationalism, at present the dominant non-Marxist approach, which is the subject of the next chapter.

But there were other, more unusual, voices that over the years have made themselves heard in the often quarrelsome family of Marxist fascist theorists. Attempts to enrich the materialist and class-based analyses of conventional Marxist-Leninist approaches to fascism with the understanding of the psychological processes involved in mass popular submission to charismatic authority led to a number of 'Freudo-Marxist' theories of its populist support. Two of them had first appeared during the ascendancy of Mussolini and Hitler but became better known after the war. In the year of Hitler's election as chancellor (1933), Wilhelm Reich published (in German) *The Mass Psychology of Fascism* (1936), which traced the roots of the general public submission to militaristic authoritarianism under both fascism and Bolshevism ('red fascism') to the acute sexual repression inflicted by conformity with the puritanical family ethic that he claimed was prevalent in modern Europe.

Reich escaped to New York in 1939. In 1941 Erich Fromm, who had emigrated to the US seven years earlier and worked at Columbia University, published *Escape from Freedom*, a study of the psychological mechanisms that had caused so many millions to find spiritual refuge in devotion to an oppressive dictatorship. Fromm, who was steeped in the scholarly study of the Talmud, blended elements of Freudo-Marxism with an idiosyncratic biblical interpretation of the expulsion of Adam and Eve from the Garden of Eden. This interpreted it as an allegory not of the Fall into Sin but of the distinctively human need to establish a morality based not on blind obedience but on inner freedom. Fromm went on to become a major spokesman for an existential humanism and the need for a 'sane' society based on 'being' and loving, not 'having' and 'owning', his works finding a receptive audience in the hippie generation.

Towards the end of the war, Theodor Adorno, another member of the Frankfurt School of Marxism, had led a research project at the University of California, Berkeley, into the propensity of 'ordinary people' to submit to the conditions of totalitarianism. This resulted in the publication of *The Authoritarian Personality* (Adorno et al. 1950), famous at the time for its proposed 'F scale', or scale of susceptibility to fascism. Original insights into the fascist mindset were also offered by a number of Marxist intellectuals concerned with the aesthetics and mythology of totalitarianism, notably Walter Benjamin ([1936] 2008) and Ernst Bloch ([1935] 2009).

Perhaps the most revealing Marxist analysis of fascism, at least for a non-Marxist, as a materialist and ideological force is to be found in the chapter 'Fascism and Ideology' by the Argentinian 'post-Marxist' Ernesto Laclau, published in his *Politics and Ideology in Marxist Theory: Capitalism, Fascism, Populism* (1977). His approach was influenced both by Gramsci's theory of cultural hegemony and by Althusser's theory of the power of radical ideology to 'interpellate' (engage on a subjective, affective level) broad strata of the disoriented in the midst of a crisis (an approach itself influenced by the French Freudo-Marxian psychologist Jacques Lacan). In Laclau's causal model, fascism's success is attributed extensively to the effectiveness of its ideology, which imbued so many who felt politically and psychologically alienated from contemporary society with the (illusory) sense of being active historical subjects endowed with a sense of collective purpose and belonging (cf. Platt 1980). This premise, which broke definitively with the materialistic explanations engendered by Marxism-Leninism and goes beyond Gramsci in recognizing the hegemony of ideology, enabled Laclau to explain fascism's power to exploit liberalism's post-1918 crises and, in some countries, to become, at least temporally, a powerful populist movement not limited to the bourgeoisie for its appeal. The masses were interpellated by fascism not as an economic class, but as a national 'people'. According to Laclau, fascism was doomed as a revolution because the ultranationalist discourse was appropriated by the bourgeoisie and turned into the reactionary defence of capitalism, a verdict that confirms Laclau's Marxist pedigree.

More recently, fresh analyses by anglophone Marxists have been advanced on fascism which also avoid simplistic equations of bourgeois reaction, capitalism and fascism, such as Neocleous (1997) and Woodley (2009). Apart from offering a sophisticated left-wing 'take' on fascism, Woodley offers a comprehensive study of the tangled history of Marxist engagement with the ideological dynamics of fascism. It is also worth mentioning the contributions by socialists of different hues to the debate on the possibility of reconciliation of Marxist and 'liberal' positions of fascism hosted by the special issue of *European Journal of Political Theory* (Roberts and Griffin 2012), which produced stimulating critiques of the limitations placed on the application of the term by 'liberal' orthodoxy (e.g. Yannielli 2012). Roger Markwick's discussion of communism's relationship to fascism (2009) is another example of how a left-wing perspective on interwar history can enrich comparative fascist studies for all concerned.

The political siren

It is clear from this survey that the hallmark of all Marxist theories of fascism, no matter how varied and nuanced, is an axiomatic assumption that capitalism either spawned fascism directly, in order to defend itself against an imminent socialist revolution, or emerged as an autonomous nationalist force with authentic counter-revolutionary elements, but could never operate as the core of a genuinely revolutionary historical process, however ephemeral. Such a premise, seen as reductionist by the theorists considered in the next chapter, underlies Bertolt Brecht's reference in his poem 'The Buddha's Parable of the Burning House', written in exile from the Third Reich in 1937, to 'the bomber squadrons of Capital', a phrase which identifies Nazism totally with capitalism. Similarly, few contemporary Marxists would disagree with the verdict which the German Ernst Bloch delivered on Nazism's socialist and revolutionary claims from exile in Switzerland in 1933 in his essay 'Inventory of Revolutionary Appearance':

> The enemy is not content with torturing and killing workers. He not only wants to smash the red front, but also strips

the jewellery off the supposed corpse. ... The burning of
the Reichstag alone is not sufficient; the populace must also
believe that Nero is the early Christian in person. Thus, is
hell mocked right from the beginning with a grotesque mask
of salvation.

Nazism, Bloch continues, has created 'a revolutionary façade
with trappings of the Paris Commune'. It is a 'false siren song',
'an illusion', 'a deception', a 'Little Red Riding Hood' who has
stolen from the communists only the 'emblems' of revolution:
'the colour red', 'the procession' and the 'dangerous songs',
'the forest of flags' (Bloch [1935] 2009: 56–63).

Eight decades later, the online *Encyclopedia of Marxism*
is still assuring its readers in the entry for 'fascism' that it is
a 'right-wing, fiercely nationalist, subjectivist in philosophy,
and totalitarian in practice. It is an extreme reactionary form
of capitalist government.' The ensuing article stresses its
pseudo-religious component, its drive to start wars in order
to create new markets, its anti-modernity, its anti-modernism,
its irrational cult of the will, and its persecution of the left,
all of which is consistent with its core nature as 'capitalism
at the stage of impotent imperialism' (*Marxists Internet
Archive Encyclopedia* 1998–2008). As we have seen, the
phrase 'Marxist theories of fascism' subsumes a rich variety
of nuanced positions, some offering important insights to
non-Marxists, but inevitably it is the more simplistic interpretations that still dominate mainstream Marxist discourse in
left-wing journalism, academic analysis and, most conspicuously, anti-fascist rallies.

The disarray of liberal historians

For non-Marxists, too, the dramatic entry of fascism onto the
stage of modern history came as a complete shock, something
that was not in the historical script of either liberals or
conservatives. In 1934, the Italian expert in German literature and aesthetics Giuseppe Borgese, who had recently
found a refuge from the Fascist regime in the New School of
Social Research in New York, wrote:

Not a single prophet, during more than a century of prophecies, analysing the degradation of the romantic culture, or planning the split of the romantic atom [*sic*], ever imagined anything like fascism. There was in the lap of the future communism and syndicalism and what not; there was anarchism, and legitimism, and even all-papacy ['pan-papism'?]; war, peace, pan-Germanism, pan-Slavism, Yellow Peril, signals to the planet Mars; there was no fascism. It came as a surprise to all, and to [fascists] themselves too. (Borgese 1934: 475–6)

In their state of intellectual bewilderment, political commentators were at a loss when it came to making sense of this brash new political force from within the framework of the dominant humanist assumptions about rational progress, individualism and civilization. As a result, the task of establishing some sort of consensus about its definitional core, sometimes referred to as the 'fascist minimum', proved considerably more intractable than it did for Marxists. Indeed, it produced a sustained Babel effect that lasted over half a century, proliferating largely incompatible and sometimes mutually incomprehensible definitions of minimal use to historians and political scientists working on specific events.

What nearly all 'liberal' attempts to resolve this problem shared with Marxist approaches, however, was the premise that a key to understanding fascism, or at least defining it, did not lie in detailed analysis of how fascists themselves saw the ultimate goals of their movement and the policies and actions needed to realize them. Instead, it was a process of identifying intuitively key features that stood out to a convinced *anti-fascist*. A parallel could be drawn with the century that passed before professional psychiatrists (as opposed to psychotherapists) finally started to take an interest in how people with diagnosed psychological 'disorders' or mental 'illnesses' actually perceive the world, an empathetic approach known significantly as 'anti-psychiatry' (e.g. Laing 1960). Their work brought to light the *alternative* rational structures of the thought processes and behavioural logics which their testimonies expose when treated 'phenomenologically' – i.e. in terms of how reality is experienced subjectively.

Until the 1990s, therefore, non-Marxist theories of fascism were characterized by an extraordinary heterogeneity, based as they were on working arbitrarily on the basis of what Alexander De Grand called an 'outside in' approach (De Grand 1996: 3). The resulting profusion of incompatible approaches is clear from contemporary surveys of them (e.g. Gregor 1974; De Felice 1977; Hagtvet and Kühnl 1980). One of the first, Luigi Salvatorelli's *Nazionalfascismo* (1924), focused on Fascism's allegedly petty bourgeois class base (conceived in a non-Marxist sense), a theme elaborated a decade later in the psychological theory of Harold Lasswell (1933) of how 'Hitlerism' addressed the psychological anxieties of the lower middle class. After the war, Seymour Lipset (1960) would then famously present fascism as the 'extremism of the middle classes' who were losing out in the rise of a modern economy and society, an approach distantly reminiscent of Bonapartist theories. They were not to know any more than Marxists that the middle-class thesis of Fascism and Nazism, routinely encountered in school history textbooks until recently, would one day be empirically refuted. This was possible thanks to the painstaking analysis by scholars, such as Jürgen Falter, Thomas Childers, Michael Kater and Detlef Mühlberger, of the sociological background (scrupulously recorded in NSDAP membership records) of those who joined the party before January 1933 (Mühlberger 1991).[3] (Once Hitler was chancellor, membership statistics no longer provided reliable evidence of genuine ideological support.) The middle-class thesis has no factual basis in any other fascisms either, all of which prove to have transclass support consisting of many social categories and constituencies, some of them predominantly rural and peasant-based (Mühlberger 1998).

A diametrically opposed approach was to see in fascism a symptom of the rise of the masses who had yet to find a secure cultural sense of identity or 'home' within modern society. As a result, they were susceptible to the delusion of being existentially and historically empowered through communal ultranationalist fervour and promises of imperial greatness. It is an approach that has affinities both with Laclau's stress on the way hundreds of thousands, millions even, can feel 'interpellated' by the heady rhetoric of imminent fascist revolution and with Fromm's analysis of the wave of mass insecurity at the height of the Wall Street Crash as the main driver of fascism. An important anticipation of such approaches was provided by José Ortega y Gasset ([1930] 1932), who, reflecting the influence of Gustave Le Bon's theory of crowd mentality and of Nietzsche's warnings about the threat posed by a new race of nihilistic 'last men', presented fascism as expressing the 'revolt of the masses' against advanced civilization. In the 1950s, both Talcott Parsons (1954) and William Kornhauser (1959) would interpret fascism not as a class phenomenon but as a mass movement of populist radicalism on a par with communism. In similar vein, Paul Brooker (1991) later applied Durkheim's theory of 'mechanical solidarity' to explain the mass enthusiasm for the militarized nation created by Italian Fascism, Nazi Germany and imperial Japan, all of which offered a strong sense of communal identity in an age of rising anomie. However, serious *ideological* analysis of how fascism conceived its revolutionary projects, or, rather, analysis that took ideology *seriously* as a vital component of the historical reality and unique political DNA of fascism, was conspicuously absent from all these works. Understanding the cluster of core myths which in the 1930s had unleashed fascism's extraordinary psychological power to mobilize elements of both the middle classes and the working-class masses (as well as of the ruling elites) through the power of ideology transmitted through sophisticated propaganda was assumed to be irrelevant.

The same is true of another approach to identifying fascism's dynamic. This focused neither on class relations, nor on mass society, but on modernization or, rather, dysfunctions in the modernization process, which was understood as an extension of the Enlightenment project of founding progress on a combination of rationally based science and socio-political institutions shaped by liberal values. Here again we find a plethora of competing explanations that can only be alluded to in such a brief survey. They range from Barrington Moore's attempt (1966) to analyse fascism as one of the (dead-end) routes from feudalism to socio-economic modernity; to Henry Turner's portrayal (1975) of fascism as paradoxically needing to embrace technological and bureaucratic modernity in a spirit of 'modernist anti-modernism' so as to re-create a socially and politically pre-modern society in modern guise; to the idea of unintentional modernization

(Schoenbaum 1966; Dahrendorf 1968); to the thesis put forward by Jeffrey Herf (1984) that Nazi technocrats embodied a 'reactionary modernism'. None was prepared to offer a concise definition of fascism, which thus remained a curiously nebulous concept in their discussions, especially in terms of its relationship to modernity and core ideological features. The most famous expert to offer a definition of fascism based on its animus against modernity was Ernst Nolte (1965), who presented it as 'resistance to theoretical and practical transcendence', where 'transcendence' can be taken to refer to a gradual process of emancipation from traditional social, economic and ideological constraints. The in-depth analysis of the Action Française, Fascism and Nazism that culminated in this definition gave new impetus to comparative fascism studies after the 1960s, even if Nolte's own definitional formula proved far too abstract and obscure to be put to practical use by researchers.

Earlier, three major books conceived at the height of Nazi power or in its immediate aftermath had memorably explored fascism from yet another angle, namely the moral nihilism and destruction of personal freedom that flowed from the Nazi regime's radical rejection of Enlightenment values. Hermann Rauschning's *The Revolution of Nihilism* (1939) warned the West that the Nazi determination to create a new order demanded the destruction of all Christian and conservative values; Hannah Arendt's *The Origins of Totalitarianism* (1951) highlighted the way Nazism and Bolshevism systematically used propaganda and terror to destroy inner freedom in order to maximize state power; while György Lukács's *The Destruction of Reason* ([1952] 1980), armed with a Marxist concept of reason, traced the genealogy of philosophical irrationalists who paved the way for the Nazi use of myth and conspiracy theories as the foundation stones of the new order.

Significantly, none of these authors showed any interest in the definitional issues posed by generic fascism, and several major historians of Mussolini's regime, notably Renzo De Felice (1976), A. J. Gregor (1979) and Zeev Sternhell (1986), would later argue that Nazism was in any case generically unrelated to Italian Fascism, and hence to any other fascism. Meanwhile, in the postwar Germanies, while Marxists continued to apply largely uncritically their Soviet concept of fascism to the NSDAP and the Third Reich, most 'liberals' preferred to follow Arendt in using the paradigm of 'totalitarianism' as the most helpful generic concept for making sense of the Third Reich (e.g. Bracher 1973; Pohlmann 2008).

A way out of the labyrinth

In short, for fifty years after the death of the dictators, non-Marxist comparative studies in fascism were in a chaotic state. The models of fascism they were generating proved too arbitrary and empirically ungrounded to help researchers working 'idiographically' (concerned with reconstructing and analysing particular phenomena and events) to recognize general patterns in their specialist area of inquiry or to distinguish between fascist and non-fascist manifestations of the extreme right. There is a fable known to Jains, Buddhists and Sufis about a village of blind men who, encountering an elephant for the first time, all picture a different animal according to which part of the creature they felt, and all adamantly assert their version as the true one.[4] For over four decades after the era of fascism had ended, most of those pursuing the chimera of generic fascism proceeded in a similar way in order to arrive at an overarching theory. They generally selected or assumed a cluster of (often negative) components common to Fascism or Nazism, or both (other fascisms were usually assumed too peripheral to be included in this process), and then treated them as the definitional core of generic fascism. Others felt entitled to write entire books about fascism without even offering a definition (e.g. Carsten 1967; De Felice 1977).

A symptom of the prevailing disarray and malaise of 'liberal' historians in the area of comparative studies of fascism was the neglect of one of the earliest books to have taken a study of its ideology as the starting point for analysis: Eugen Weber's *Varieties of Fascism* (1964). Despite its considerable methodological and conceptual clarity, accessibility to students and concision, it fell into obscurity. Meanwhile, as we have pointed out, Nolte's conceptually demanding and opaque *Three Faces of Fascism*, published in an English edition almost contemporaneously with Weber's book, achieved international fame, despite being a dead end for practical research purposes. A deep-seated bias against taking fascist texts seriously as a source of understanding the fascist world-view and goals, and thereby the politics and actions derived from them (something Weber had grasped), meant that historians and political scientists continued to publish on individual fascisms, but without any sense of contributing to a collaborative enterprise or of belonging to a mature sub-discipline of the historical and political sciences. The result was a steady proliferation of rival approaches often based on external features, several of which (e.g. charismatic leadership, terror, racism, the single party state, ritual politics, corporatism, extreme nationalism, apocalyptic imagery) were in no way peculiar to the extreme right. As a consequence, 'fascist studies' were largely (and rightly) ignored by historians and political scientists for all practical research purposes.

Another symptom of this sorry state of affairs was that compilations of essays on fascism designed to help students could offer little more than a motley collection of divergent analyses useless for the definitional and taxonomic require-ments of comparative studies (e.g. Woolf 1968; Laqueur 1976; Larsen et al. 1980). Meanwhile, monographs on a particular national fascism had no broadly consensual definition to invoke as corroboration or justification of the approach used (e.g. Hamilton 1971; Soucy 1986; Thurlow 1987). The dilemma was most acute for the compliers of political dictionaries, who at times found themselves reduced to offering nonsensical observations of minimal use for identifying a movement as fascist or not, such as 'fascism had the form of an ideology without the content' and was 'an amalgam of disparate conceptions, often ill-understood, often bizarre' (Scruton 1983: 244–5). So desperate was the situation that Stuart Woolf, who in 1967 held the major international conference at Reading University on individual fascisms on which the chapters of his book *The Nature of Fascism* were based, actually suggested in his introduction that 'Perhaps the word fascism should be banned, at least temporarily, from our political vocabulary' (Woolf 1968: 132; cf. Allardyce 1979: 370).

Equally telling was the opening sentence of a pamphlet published by the UK's Historical Association in 1981 entitled *Fascism in Europe*. It was presumably intended as a clarification of the concept, yet its opening sentence warned readers that, 'Although enormous amounts of research time and mental energy have been put into the study of it ..., fascism has stubbornly remained the great conundrum for students of the twentieth century' (Robinson 1981: 1). In the same vein, a review of the first major collection of essays on the sociology of fascism, *Who Were the Fascists?* (Larsen et al. 1980), opened with the observation: 'Perhaps one day someone will formulate a universally acceptable definition of fascism and will clearly identify the fascists, but that day still seems far off' (Deák 1983: 13). For undergraduates and postgraduates outside the Marxist tradition undertaking work on fascism, such a lack of consensus posed serious problems. Every book consulted opened another door leading into a new corridor in the seemingly endless and centreless labyrinth of partly conflicting, but sometimes tantalizingly convergent, approaches that had become the outstanding feature of fascist studies.

Yet the breakthrough that Deák hoped for came about much sooner than he could have imagined. Naturally, a universally accepted definition of fascism is neither possible (because of the basic mismatch between any single concept and an infinitely variegated external reality, which forces every political term to be a construct) nor desirable (because it would mean the end of academic freedom and scientific progress). But a significant degree of consensus among academic experts on a fruitful approach to comparative fascist studies was about to emerge. No definitional Holy Grail or hidden seam of gold was about to be found in the manner of an Indiana Jones film. But ever more academics came to understand that it was possible after all to identify fascism's 'black cat' in a room once it was no longer darkened by methodological naivety but illuminated by the realization that 'fascism' is not an objective 'thing' to be found or defined. Rather, like all other political concepts, it is a heuristic device which can be articulated as a working definition, not definitive but at least definite, on the basis of solid comparative and collaborative research which encourages complementary studies to be carried out in the future.

The outstanding feature of the 'new wave' of fascist studies that first made its presence felt in the early 1990s was a subtle but significant change in perspective from the view of an opponent or victim to that of the protagonists themselves (which is the standard approach to other political concepts, such as conservatism, liberalism, socialism, feminism, ecologism). This 'paradigm shift' at last enabled researchers to engage directly with fascists through their political, historical and humanistic imagination as a species of political actor motivated by a particular genus of world-view, ideology and utopian programme for the transformation of society. On this basis, fascist ideology would no longer be approached as a façade to euphemize cynical material and class interests or the poisonous fruit of destructive hatred and fanaticism. Instead, 'methodological empathy' now revealed it as the expression, albeit a generally propagandistic one, of deeply held beliefs and emotionally and mythically powerful ideals about what is wrong with society and what should be done to regenerate it, to bring about a total renewal of its culture in an anthropological sense. As George Mosse, the pioneer of this approach, put it: 'the cultural interpretation of fascism opens up a means to penetrate fascist self-understanding, and such empathy is crucial in order to grasp how people saw the movement' (Mosse 1999: xi).

Few fascists would have been aware of the deep-structural causes and the immediate confluence of external and internal factors feeding not only their hatreds and fears but also their utopian dreams of an ultranationalist revolution. But how they evaluated the existential threat to their society and identity in the midst of the interwar or postwar crisis of the nation, and the draconian measures they proposed in order to resolve it, expressed their own psychological truths in a particular ideological form. This was sufficiently distinct from other political projects finally to allow those studying fascism to define it coherently on a par with other political concepts, namely in terms primarily of its positive ideals and not the negations or 'anti'-dimension which flowed from these ideals (Payne 1995: 5–7). At this point, the 'fascist conundrum' could begin to resolve itself, the Gordian knot tied by decades of uncoordinated study could loosen, and researchers could finally set to work without agonizing over their own definitions and other experts' conflicting theories. A coherent account of the characteristic world-view and ideology of fascists based on their own understanding of them, while utterly rejecting the rationality and morality of the policies and actions that flowed from them, started to establish itself as the norm, at least within academic studies.

As a result of this unexpected development, texts which Marxists would (still) dismiss as a propagandist smokescreen of nationalist fervour put up to conceal the terroristic exploitation of the masses by capitalism, or in which liberals could see little more than the bombastic rhetoric of a megalomaniac leader who managed to seize power only thanks to the chaotic aftermath of the First World War, suddenly take on a deeper significance. For example, with the seventh anniversary of victory in the First World War only days away, Mussolini, in his first year as *duce*, addressed the National Association of War-Wounded, precisely the constituency of veterans whose patriotism and courage he looked to as constituting what he called the 'trenchocracy' (Griffin 1995: 28–9), the heroic, youthful elite on which a new type of modern Italy would be based. He used the occasion to share with his listeners his 'big idea', a vision that energized Fascism, and whose many equivalents can be seen as the animating force of all fascisms.

Italy's glorious history and impact on civilization, he told them, had not ended with the creation of the Roman Empire, the establishment of the Roman Catholic Church, or the rebirth of the West's Classical heritage in the Renaissance that flowed from its heart. With the foundation of the Fascist State, Italy was about to offer yet another gift to the world as the creator of a new phase of civilization:

> The fatherland is no illusion! It is the sweetest, greatest, most human, most divine of realities! No! Italy did not exhaust herself in creating its first and second civilization, but is already creating a third. Fellow soldiers! We will create it in the name of the king, in the name of Italy, with physical effort, with the spirit, with blood and with life. (Mussolini 1925)

When Hitler became chancellor, the prospect of national regeneration inspired similarly ecstatic sentiments in Nazi supporters, who believed they were witnessing the rebirth of their nation, so recently brought to its knees by a series of crises. One of them recorded his hopes for Germany's metamorphosis during the 'seizure of power' in a book dedicated to 'the longing for the Third Reich': 'Tomorrow has become today: the feeling that the world is ending has given way to the sense of a new beginning. The ultimate goal now stands out unmistakably within the field of vision now opening up before us, and all faith in miracles is now harnessed to the active transformation of the present' (Petersen 1934: 1).

The empathetic approach advocated by Mosse suggests that such passages are certainly to be read as propaganda – not in the sense of cynical manipulation but rather as attempts to disseminate a faith, true to the word's origin in the Vatican's 'Sacred Congregation for the Propagation of the Faith' (Sacra Congregatio de Propaganda Fide), formed in 1622 and dissolved only in 1922. Once the cornerstone of this faith within fascist 'self-understanding' is recognized through methodological empathy as the imminent rebirth of the nation or race in a post-liberal new order, such primary texts act as signposts to the second main route taken by researchers in their attempt to make sense of fascism, which is the subject of the next chapter.

3

A Working Definition: Fascism as a Revolutionary Form of Nationalism

A third way to understand fascism

Having considered the relatively coherent Marxist and, for a time, chronically incoherent liberal attempts within academia to pin down or, rather, collaboratively decide on the elusive fascist minimum, this chapter offers readers a definite (rather than definitive) conceptual framework or 'research paradigm' for studying generic fascism as a key concept in political thought. As explained at the end of the last chapter, the 'third approach' which it represents is based on the increasingly accepted principle of applying empathy methodologically 'to penetrate fascist self-understanding' (Mosse 1999: xi) in order to resolve the tangled definitional conundrum that fascism poses. The reason why it is presented here as a 'working definition' is that, outside the Marxist tradition, it is the explanatory model that has so far proven to have the greatest heuristic value for researching fascism, as demonstrated by the abundance of articles, chapters and books produced since the 1990s which apply it, whether explicitly or not. In other words, the definition expounded here, based on prioritizing the testimonies, whether in the words, policies, actions, institutional innovations or cultural products, of fascists themselves in order to understand the inner logic of their ideology and actions, is the one which to date has actually been shown to 'work' best.

Adopting this conceptual approach does not, of course, mean that academics should suspend their professional analytical skills when attempting to understand the objective social and psychological factors and complex historical causes that led (and lead) to the emergence of a specific fascist ideology and its adoption in the first place. Naturally, those committed to fascism were and are largely oblivious of such factors and causes and can give only mythicized, value-laden rationalizations of their adoption of their cause, just as all historical actors can have only limited introspection about the networks of causality actually shaping their lives and motivating their ideas and behaviour at any one moment. Nor does 'methodological empathy' absolve academics from the duty of applying the very humanistic values, secular or religious, which were so alien to fascists themselves when assessing the impact and wider consequences of their belief system and policies as historical and moral forces. In particular, humanistic values are vital in motivating the historian's ambition to give full, empirically grounded and theoretically coherent accounts of fascism, of the systemic crimes against humanity and horrific unintended consequences which resulted from the most ruthless attempts to realize fascist utopias before 1945 that claimed so many millions of lives.

Such values should also inform the collective academic enterprise of monitoring and analysing how fascism has evolved since 1945, especially since the application of the working definition to its postwar manifestations often calls for finely nuanced distinctions between different species of extreme right which could appear to an outsider unnecessarily pedantic and legalistic. The specialist language and abstract classifications or theories routinely encountered in fascist studies should not be taken as a sign of indifference to the highly personal suffering and tragedy caused by every instance of fascist violence, any more than the technical language of a journal of oncology implies a lack of care for the patient suffering from cancer. In particular, the highly condensed and schematic account of the postwar evolution of fascism in chapter 5 should not divert attention from the tradition of militant xenophobia, homophobia, misogyny, homicidal violence and, in some cases, even plans for genocide (now reduced to utopian fantasy) which have resulted from the persistent attempts of fanatics long after the fascist epoch ended to realize dreams of a new national or racial order. It is to make such phenomena more humanly intelligible that this book has been written, not to reduce them to abstract definitions.

In short, methodological empathy is only a strategy adopted to enter the affective, subjective world-view and value-system of the protagonists of fascism. Leo Tolstoy declared in his *War and Peace* (1868) that 'Tout comprendre, c'est tout pardoner', but in the context of fascist studies the reverse is true: to understand fascism empathetically as a historical and political force is *not* to accept its values, justify its actions, or deny the unimaginable scale of atrocities and crimes against humanity to which the bid to implement its ideals have led in practice. The result is the sort of 'double think' familiar to sociologists, anthropologists and modern psychiatrists regarding the human protagonists under investigation, who become simultaneously subject and object of their inquiry. It is worth emphasizing in this context that 'empathetic' does not mean 'intuitive' or 'subjective' with regard to primary source data. No matter how schematic or arbitrary the interpretations of fascist ideology that result from the empathetic approach may seem, they are all based, if not on first-hand, then at least on second-hand empirical research into texts (in the widest possible sense) that document the fascists' own perception of their mission to renew the race or nation and the actions needed to accomplish it.[1]

The rest of this guide to fascist studies will build on the account of generic fascist ideology expounded in this chapter. In chapter 4 the focus will be on its implications for research into individual permutations of the interwar revolutionary right, highlighting both the remarkable core consistency and yet extreme heterogeneity of what it identifies as fascist movements once attention moves to specific ideological, social, economic, political or cultural phenomena. Chapter 5 will concentrate instead on showing how the core fascist vision identified by the empathetic approach has been able to outlast the defeat of fascist regimes in the Second World War.

Despite being successfully marginalized by liberal democracy, thanks to its capacity to generate a number of new organizational forms, propaganda strategies and ideological forms, fascism has continued to survive in a climate generally hostile to genuinely revolutionary forms of nationalism and racism.

Palingenetic ultranationalism

The account given here of fascism is one of a number of congruent approaches and definitions based on the principle of methodological empathy which understands it in terms of the core values, political diagnoses and ultimate goals of the fascists themselves (notably Payne 1995: 14; Eatwell 1995: 11; Gregor 1999: 162, 166; Blinkhorn 2000: 115–16; Shenfield 2001: 17; Kallis 2003; Mann 2004: 13; Lyons [1997] 2016; Morgan 2003: 13–14; Paxton 2007: 218; Iordachi 2009). My own formulation of the working definition of fascism proposed in this chapter makes use of the term *palingenesis* – from the Greek *palin* (again) and *genesis* (birth) – to refer to the fascists' vision of imminent or eventual rebirth. This word may well be unfamiliar to English-speaking students, even if it is current in Latin languages such as Italian and Spanish. However, since it was first introduced in *The Nature of Fascism* (Griffin 1991: 34–40) to solve the lexical problem posed by the absence of an adjective derived from the term 'rebirth', it has been widely taken up within the comparative fascist studies community and beyond, especially in its adjectival form, *palingenetic*. Subsequently, its existence as a 'real' word in political science has been acknowledged by no less an authority than *The Oxford English Dictionary* (not to mention *Wikipedia*!).

When either 'palingenetic' or 'revolutionary' are used in the context of fascist studies, it points to a major shift away both from mainstream Marxist approaches, which deny fascism a genuine revolutionary status as an ideology, and from earlier liberal approaches, which tended to characterize fascism in terms of its negations (irrational, illiberal, anti-socialist, anti-humanist, anti-modern, pathological, etc.). If readers wonder why in the context of fascism it is not preferable simply to use the far more familiar (but even more contested) political term 'revolution' instead of 'palingenesis', it is because arguably (i.e. I argue that) revolutionary theory and actions can be seen as the manifestations of structurally deeper psychological drivers and ideological forces at work in shaping their protagonists' goals and activism than exclusively political utopianism. What predates and conditions the commitment to a new order is (I suggest) a visceral longing for radical change and regeneration which can be explained only partially by objective socio-political forces of crisis and has a deep symbolic and psychological dimension. It was an aspect of political myth that particularly interested the French political thinker Georges Sorel (Ohana 1991). The profound psychological longing for cleansing, for renewal through 'creative destruction', can be seen expressed in the regenerative myths and utopian visions of a totally new society and the creation of a 'new man'[2] encountered in the French (Ozouf 1989), Bolshevik (Pellicani 2003), Maoist (Haglund 1975) and Khmer Rouge (e.g. Ponchaud 1978) revolutions, all of which were in the long run no less abortive than fascism's own revolutionary undertakings in the interwar period (and two of which were proportionately no less destructive of human life).

Palingenetic expectancy projected onto the nation or race is thus presented in my own version of the ideal type as a key psychological driver of fascist violence and *precedes* the formulation of the transformative mission and specific policies in socio-political terms. The longing for total renewal continues to shape postwar fascism, but, now its populist base has collapsed, many forms of it have been forced to pursue a hidden agenda, deliberately concealing the illiberal, totalizing or violent implications of achieving their ultimate goal. This is done in order for fascist extremism to be accommodated in an age in which revolutionary nationalism is still overwhelmingly discredited by association with the horrors of the Second World War.

In my particular version of this third approach to fascism, 'palingenetic' is paired not with the term 'nationalism' but with 'ultranationalism' (Griffin 1991: 26–55). The intended significance of the prefix 'ultra' here (meaning 'beyond' in Latin) is that the imagined community, the 'nation', so central to the fascist mindset, has moved irrevocably beyond the spectrum of social ideals compatible with liberal democracy. In the process, nationalism, even if it preserves a façade of democratic legitimacy, has been shorn of any humanistic or egalitarian connotations that it can acquire in a liberal or a socialist context as a source of communal individual, civic and legal freedoms and rights. Fascist 'ultranationalism' thus viscerally rejects 'liberal nationalism'. Within the fascist vision of the world, the nation is often reified (turned into a real entity) and personified to the point where it can be 'sick', 'decadent', 'humiliated' or 'desecrated', but it can also be 'healthy', 'strong', 'reborn', 'glorious', 'sacred'. It should be noted, however, that the organic concept of the nation can also occur in a non-fascist context, for example in the Classical Roman concept of 'the eternal city', the notion of the Jews as an 'eternal nation', and in any extreme form patriotism which holds that those who die for the national cause are 'martyrs' to a transcendental, sacred cause and in their deaths transcend personal mortality (Buc 2015). This myth was central to ensuring the human hecatombs of ritual sacrifice to all the nations who participated in the First World War continued inexorably until over 10 million combatants were dead and another 20 million seriously wounded.

It is important to note that, while in the interwar period the fascist 'ultra-nation' (if the neologism can be permitted) was overwhelmingly identified with the nation-state as the context and framework for national rebirth, even then myths of imperialism, pan-Slavism, pan-Latinity, a new European order, a Greater Germanic Reich and a rejuvenated Western civilization occasionally extended the core entity at the heart of the fascist's imagined community and sense of belonging far beyond the historical and geographical contours of the political nation-state. In particular, at least as long as the European empire was expanding, the pervasive Aryan myth of National Socialism, combined with the vision of the Third Reich as both the custodian of Nordic blood and culture and the architect of a vast new civilization based on race with its centre in a rebuilt Berlin (to be known as Germania), spawned grandiose imaginings of national community[3] and racial destiny which could assume globalizing elements (Thies 2012). After 1945, European and international reworkings of palingenetic myth and the spectacular rise of white supremacism, accompanied by the decline of the nation-state and the rise of supranational bodies and globalization, have detached fascism ever more frequently from a restricted 'nation-statism' and turned Nazism from a Germany-centred movement into a global creed of white racists, termed by some 'Universal Nazism' (see chapter 5).

The ability of the ultra-nation to have connotations both of a regenerated nation-state and of a reborn civilization or race, sometimes simultaneously, gives this component of the central fascist myth, or 'fascist minimum' – what the theorist Michael Freeden (1996) would call its 'ineliminable core' – particular flexibility and affective appeal in the context of palingenetic longings at the time of crisis. As an emotive force, and as a source of identity and purpose, the strength of fascist ideology often lies in the nebulousness and utopian quality of its vision, not in its practicality or realizability. Thus the fact that fanatically patriotic neo-fascists from different countries may attend international rallies (e.g. the annual jamboree at Diksmuide in Belgium) or conferences (e.g. the one hosted by the International Russian Conservative Forum in St Petersburg in March 2015) is a paradox, but certainly no contradiction.

The fascist ultra-nation can be envisaged as a supra-individual product of the fascist imagination which can partake of aspects of both the historical 'motherland' and 'fatherland', but also of mythicized historical and racial pasts and future destinies. It provides the mythic focal point for the fascist to feel part of a supra-personal community of belonging, identity and shared culture (whether based on history, language, territory, religion or blood, or a mixture of several such components). It is into this mystic entity that the individual is encouraged to submerge his or her tormented, angry, disoriented self entirely, thus dissolving it into an 'identificatory community' rather than forming part of an 'integrative community', one which respects the difference, individualism and humanity of 'the Other' (Griffin 1994). In some respects, the 'ultra-nation' also takes on aspects of the Judeo-Christian God: it lives both in and through the unfolding of historical time and, contemporaneously, in the supra-historical eternity of the people or race. Moreover, in extreme situations – when the 'motherland' is threatened or the 'fatherland' commands it – it may demand love, commitment and suffering from the faithful literally to the point of the ultimate sacrifice, thus making their life holy through death while further sanctifying the ultra-nation.

On a psychological level, identification with the 'ultra-nation' can thus serve as a portal to transcendence for individuals whose personal lives have been shattered by socio-political and economic upheavals that threaten their core identity as individuals, or whose inner lives might otherwise be experienced as devoid of purpose, meaning and hope because of the personal crises they are experiencing. Heroic service to this supra-personal entity enables them to enter its highly mythicized story, its history, and perhaps fleetingly know directly the sensation of redemption and immortality evoked in the sacred texts and rituals of military burial and commemoration ceremonies dedicated to fallen soldiers all over the world (Mosse 1990). It should be noted, however, that the two world wars proved that, at times of national danger, even liberal democratic nation-states can develop intense, elaborate and at least partially spontaneous political religions centred on the moral imperative of individual 'blood' sacrifice to the national community (e.g. Marvin and Ingle 1999). The difference is that liberal societies do not abandon civil nationalism and political liberalism as the basis of the ideal social order to which life should return after the crisis (Gentile 2006). In contrast, fascism sees the sacralized nation that may emerge under democracy *in extremis* at a time of national emergency and war not as an exceptional state, but as the inauguration of a new societal norm. Where liberal constraints were removed in the 1930s and 1940s, fascism attempted to engineer a sustained climate of extreme patriotism, reinforced in some cases by terror, which demanded the selflessness and sacrifice of a whole generation as the precondition for the replacement of 'sick' liberal democracy by a 'healthy' totalitarian new order inhabited, once the wars were over, by a socially engineered population of believers purged of theological, humanist or individual conscience.

It is implicit in this account that, following an early modern tradition of conceiving the subjects of a regime as constituting a 'body politic', whether autonomously self-regulating (as posited by Francisco Suárez) or created from above (as proposed by Thomas Hobbes), the fascist imagination turns 'the people' into an intrinsically anti-democratic and anti-egalitarian, *organic* entity signified by such words as 'Volk' (German), 'volk' (Dutch), 'narod' (Croatian) or 'poporul' (Romanian). However, it is important not to infer from this that fascism is inherently *biologically* or *genetically* racist. Certainly, any organic concept of the nation is intrinsically racist in the way it tends to treat ethnicities or nationalities as idealized singular entities which are threatened by miscegenation (ethnic mixing), mass migration, cosmopolitanism, materialism, individualism or absorption into international bodies. Yet, as will become apparent in chapter 4, the ultra-nation of the fascist political imagination is not necessarily racist in biological, pseudo-scientific or eugenic terms. Nor is it necessarily obsessed with 'blood-lines', racial purity or heredity. Nor is it necessarily 'eliminationist' (Goldhagen 2007), or genocidal (Kallis 2008) in the manner of Nazism, the Iron Guard or the Ustasha, in its treatment of other nationalities, ethnicities and out-groups.

From what has been said earlier about the way the fascist 'ultra-nation' is not necessarily equated with the nation-state, it is also clear that fascist ultranationalism does not preclude tactical alliances being forged with other ultranationalisms in a common *supranational* cause to fight the same international forces of ideological hostility or decadence held to be destroying the organic nation. Ultranationalism, despite its primary stress on the need for national or racial palingenesis, can thus acquire an important international or transnational dimension beyond narrow cultural, linguistic and ethnic divides, a fact being increasingly recognized by fascist studies (see chapter 6).

A one-sentence definition of fascism

On the basis of what has been said above, the one-sentence definition originally formulated in my *The Nature of Fascism* will hopefully make sense, despite the highly condensed way in which 'concrete individual phenomena' relating to fascism have been 'arranged into a unified analytical construct' or 'thought-picture' consistent with Max Weber's original ideal type theory (see chapter 1, note 2): 'Fascism is a genus of political ideology whose mythic core in its various permutations is a palingenetic form of populist ultranationalism' (Griffin 1991: 26). Unpacked, this formulation offers the following solution to the 'conundrum' posed by fascism as a political concept to newcomers to the field or fellow researchers not pre-armed with their own theory:

a) generic fascism should be treated on a par with other **political ideologies** which refer to thinkers, movements, regimes, policies or actions motivated by the prospect of realizing a particular vision of the ideal society and set of political and cultural values on which it is based;
b) as with other generic political ideologies, fascism manifests itself in a wide variety of forms, some extremely diverse, and can be imagined as forming a vast extended family of related **permutations** of the same ideal type;
c) the inner coherence of fascism as a generic concept emerges once these different permutations are interpreted in relation to a **core utopian myth** of an ideal state of society and civilization and the practical consequences of attempting to translate that myth into practice in a particular historical context;
d) the core myth, ideal-typically constructed, is that an organic 'people' forming an '**ultra-nation**' is in crisis and needs to be saved from its present state of disintegration and decadence through the agency of a vanguard made up of those who are keenly aware of the current forces that threaten it and are prepared to fight to combat them (though, especially in the postwar period, this 'fight' may not necessarily be physical or violent);
e) the definitional minimum of generic fascism is thus that it embraces an ideology, and its related policies and practices, centred on the need to mobilize **populist** energies of renewal (**palingenesis**) to bring about the rebirth of the ultra-nation, thereby inaugurating a new, revolutionary national or civilizational order.

If this explanation still comes across as extremely convoluted and unnecessarily abstract, the following chapters will hopefully put some empirical and historical flesh on the definitional skeleton. However, it may not be until students (in the widest sense) wrestle with particular fascist regimes, movements and phenomena, or with theoretical issues relating to them, that the approach presented here for using fascism as a 'key political concept' may suddenly spring into life. If it still seems at this stage abstruse and usable for essay or research purposes, it is probably a sign that some more work is necessary in this direction.

Mosse's application of methodological empathy to fascist studies

The 'empathetic' understanding of fascism as a positive vision of a new society has a protracted pre-history. We have already seen that some Marxist theorists, notably Gramsci and later Vajda, conceded that there was an element of radicalness and innovation in the fascists' onslaught against liberal democracy which gained some genuine populist traction even within the 'proletariat'. A now largely forgotten non-Marxist commentator who came to a similar conclusion early on was Erwin von Beckerath, whose *Wesen und Werden des faschistischen Staates* (Essence and Development of the Fascist State, 1927) already saw in Mussolini's regime, then barely two years old, a creative attempt to combine elements of eighteenth-century absolutism with a new kind of modern authoritarian state as a total solution to the chronic problems of liberal Italy.

More famous, but no more influential on later historiography, was *The End of Economic Man: A Study of the New Totalitarianism* (1939) by the future guru of US management theory, Peter Drucker. This neglected classic presented the establishment of Fascism and Nazism as attempts to resolve the existential crisis of modern society in the interwar period by replacing the morally bankrupt (fascists would add 'decadent') liberal age of *'homo economicus'*, a human type motivated by the individualistic pursuit of economic self-interest, with a new age based on *'homo heroicus'*. This new species of human being would live out modernity not in the materialistic spirit of instrumental reason but in a communal spirit of extreme vitalism. Drucker's prediction was more in tune with the Wagnerian ethos of Norse mythology or Ernst Jünger's prophecy of the appearance of a new race of warriors (Jünger 1922) and heroic workers (Jünger 1932) than with the economic rationalism of John Maynard Keynes or Henry Ford.

The first sustained and coherent attempt to understand fascism in terms of the discernible common denominators of contrasting fascist visions of renewal, or, to use his phrase, their 'dreams' of a new world, was made by George Mosse in the inaugural issue of the *Journal of Contemporary History* in 1966. In hindsight, the first number of what was to become one of the most prestigious journals of its kind antici- pated a new era in fascist studies that was to come to fruition three decades later. It is dedicated to 'international fascism', and individual articles discuss movements and ideologues in France, Italy, Romania, Norway, Russia and Spain, thus fully recognizing fascism's existence as a generic concept which manifests in a variety of permutations. But it is Mosse's essay on 'The Genesis of Fascism' (1966a), published two years after Eugen Weber's *Varieties of Fascism* almost surrepti- tiously cracked the mould in comparative fascist studies, that is so strikingly ground-breaking.

In it, Mosse depicts interwar fascism exclusively in terms that its own protagonists and militants themselves would understand, namely as a dual spiritual revolt, both against the nihilism of a bourgeois morality that had 'dissolved into nothingness' with the catastrophic events of the First World War and their aftermath and against the atomization and alienation promoted by the egotistic individualism and materialism of liberal modernity. By locating the deeper ideological roots of fascism in the late nineteenth-century 'revolt against positivism', he is able to recognize its struc- tural links with the Expressionists' celebration of instinct and 'the soul' in their 'urge to recapture the "whole man"' in drama, painting and poetry. Mosse is also prepared to evoke empathetically the dynamism of the fascist experience of reality as a futural, *joyful* process, an insight which is utterly obscured when the perspective of opponents and victims is prioritized as the basis of understanding. Only because he sought to reconstitute not just fascism's ideology but the tonality of the vitalistic world-view, or *Weltanschauung*, that underlay it could Mosse declare that 'all European fascisms gave the impression that the movement was open-ended, a continuous Nietzschean ecstasy'. Fascism, he continues, strove to replace the 'chaos of the soul' bred by modernity with 'a new sense of community', bound together by a 'new religion' that 'leaned on a Christian tradition', at whose core lay the celebration of the emergence of a 'new man': 'man made whole once more, aware of his archetype and of those with whom he shared it, an activist in that he was not afraid to join in a revolution which would make society correspond to the longings of his soul.' Six decades on, Mosse might have written about the *palingenetic* longings of the new man and woman.

The spread of the new paradigm

Swimming powerfully against the dominant currents of thought in the Marxist and liberal academic arenas of the day, Mosse's article recognizes explicitly the central role to be played in conceptualizing fascism's ideology and practice effectively by focusing *empathetically* on its vision of imminent national renewal and cultural palingenesis. Furthermore, the same article wholeheartedly embraces the thesis that the concerted bid to realize this vision at all costs requires fascism to be seen as an *alternative* revolution to its arch-enemy Bolshevism. Yet Mosse himself emphasizes that this was no open-ended myth of total renewal. It was not conditioned, as for Bolsheviks, by the imperative of gaining 'control over the means of production' and building a socialist society from scratch. Instead it was shaped by the imperative of realizing the national community, a community bound together by what fascists saw as the nation's 'eternal' (or what Mosse calls 'traditional') values, by a shared, historically rooted world-view and identity, and by the mystical, exhilarating power of belonging to the Nation – in my terminology, the 'ultra-nation' – which is conceived as an organism shaped by a common history, culture and race (though not necessarily in the biological or eugenic sense).

Almost for the first time, fascism is being defined by a non-fascist in terms of its own positive ideal of the future. Mosse himself stresses: 'The fascist revolution cannot be understood if we see it merely in negative terms or judge it entirely by the dominance which national-socialism [Nazism] achieved over it by the late 1930s. For millions, it did satisfy a deeply-felt need for activism combined with identification, it seemed to embody their vision of a classless society.' Mosse clearly recognizes in this passage that fascism's psychological driver in the 1930s was an affectively powerful myth of belonging: 'The acceptance of the irrational seemed to give man roots within his inner self, while at the same time making him member of a spontaneous, not artificial, community' (Mosse 1966a).

With 'The Genesis of Fascism', Mosse laid at least in principle a solid foundation for the palingenetic paradigm of generic fascism, though it had to wait another three decades to come into its own. In two recent publications he had already applied to the Third Reich what he called his 'anthropological' understanding of fascism's core myth, as dictating the endeavour to enact a particular cosmology in an attempted total cultural revolution which conditioned the social and political changes enacted by the Nazis, and even their racial policies and genocide (Mosse 1964, 1966b). He later followed up this series of publications with an important study of the nineteenth-century development of nationalism as a new political religion which prepared the ground for Nazism (Mosse 1975) and with a collection of essays whose introduction he used to call for a velvet revolution in fascist studies based on methodological empathy with how the fascists themselves conceived their revolution (Mosse 1979). One of his last publications was a selection of articles which together highlight how consistent he had been in his analysis of the revolutionary drive behind generic fascism for over four decades (Mosse 1999). A recurrent theme in this corpus of seminal texts is fascism's bid to create a 'new man' and 'new woman', what Emilio Gentile (2005) calls its attempted 'anthropological revolution', which is only now being given its due weight in comparative studies as one of the key components of fascist totalitarianism (Feldman et al. 2017). Mosse's final work, *Confronting History* (2000), stresses the central role of empathy in the craft of the historian.

Yet, as we saw in the last chapter, despite such a potentially ground-breaking series of contributions to comparative fascist studies, Mosse's impact on the research in this area was initially minimal: international conferences continued to be organized and book introductions written as if 'fascism' was still a definitional riddle. However, all was not lost. Though their distinctive voices were also drowned out in the general cacophony surrounding the concept of fascism, by the 1970s several major researchers were pursuing independently lines of inquiry into fascism which were convergent with Mosse's approach. In Germany, for example, Klaus Vondung (1971) was investigating the sacred spaces and elaborate liturgies through which the Nazis celebrated a rebirth of Germany demanding devotion and sacrifice. Meanwhile, Klaus Theweleit (1987, 1991) had devised a remarkably widely documented psychoanalytic theory of the dynamics of Nazi fanaticism that focused on the central role in conversions to Nazism played by incomplete individuation (the process of becoming a whole person). This resulted in the existence of many thousands of men in Weimar Germany who were inwardly 'not-yet-born', but who felt fully realized and empowered once outwardly transformed by their party uniform, both material and ideological, a process which enabled them to execute orders as fanatical Nazis.

In Italy, another 'loner', the historian Emilio Gentile, despite the incomprehension of many of his colleagues, was engaged in a sustained process of reinterpreting the origins of Fascism in the dysfunctional aspects of the belated Italian unification process known as the Risorgimento, the acute cultural crisis of turn-of-the-century Italy, and the deep socio-economic and political crisis that followed the First World War (Gentile 1972). The widely diffused sense of backwardness and inferiority these generated, cumulatively combined with a nationwide identity crisis, fuelled longings in the more patriotic, anti-communist strata of society for a process of national renewal to be brought about through the emergence of a heroic generation of Nietzschean 'new men' (Gentile 1975), led by a charismatic national leader (Gentile 1976) at the head of an entirely new kind of national state (Gentile 1982).

There were several variants of the Fascist vision of the new order, which ranged from embracing Italy's Roman past to celebrating technological progress in the spirit of Filippo Marinetti's futurism, and with varying emphasis on the importance of rural life, the city, technology, culture and empire. But what all the variants of Fascism shared, as Gentile demonstrated through painstaking empirical and archival study of Fascist primary sources, was the vision of Italy finally reversing centuries of decline, backwardness and submission to foreigners and entering a phase of renaissance, creativity and strength in every sphere of national life. The resulting palingenesis (the word Gentile himself uses) manifested itself as much in the building of motorways and new towns as in the creation of youth organizations, schemes to increase the birth rate, or the creation of an 'African' empire.

Towards a new wave of collaboration in fascist studies

In the period that Deák (1983) pronounced his gloomy verdict on the prospects for definitional consensus in fascist studies, Gentile's pioneering work on Fascism was being complemented by Pier-Giorgio Zunino, who had been busy reconstituting Fascist ideology from many hundreds of primary sources which once would have been dismissed either as a smokescreen for capitalist exploitation of the masses or as cynical propaganda to justify Mussolini's ideology-less personal dictatorship. Prominent among these was the conviction that Fascism was shepherding Italians from an age of 'progressive decadence, of decline, of decomposition' to 'the era of a new civilization whose essence no one could know'. The establishment of Mussolini's regime thus marked the 'beginning of a new cycle' in history, 'the dawn of a new epoch': a heroic national response to an objective historical crisis with global consequences (Zunino 1985: 133–5).

It was in these years that Zeev Sternhell, the Israeli expert on the French far right, published his own remarkably full and original account of generic fascist ideology in

Walter Laqueur's *Fascism: A Reader's Guide: Analyses, Interpretations, Bibliography,* at the time one of the few attempts to offer readers a lucid analysis of fascism as a genus of political thought (Sternhell 1976). He later summarized the insights of this chapter in an encyclopaedia entry (Sternhell 1987) in which, unwittingly corroborating Mosse's *Journal of Contemporary History* article of 1966, he defined fascism 'as a revolutionary movement' that originated in a spirit of anti-bourgeois revolt. For Sternhell, one of the defining features of fascism was that its cult of 'organic nationalism' became synthesized with 'anti-Marxist socialism' to produce an ideology that offered 'a rejection of materialism – liberalism, democracy and Marxism being regarded simply as different aspects of the same materialist evil'. Another was that this cult was directed towards 'laying the foundations of a new civilization' at the core of which lay the experience of belonging to a new national community:

> Only a new communal and anti-individualistic civilization was deemed capable of assuring the permanence of a human collectivity in which all strata and all classes of society would be perfectly integrated, and the natural framework for such a harmonious, organic collectivity was held to be the nation – a nation enjoying a moral unity which liberalism and Marxism, both agents of warfare and disunity, could never provide. (Ibid.: 148)

The continuing idiosyncrasy of fascist theories in this period is exemplified by the fact that, whereas for George Mosse (1966a) Nazism represents the most complete embodiment of generic fascism, for Sternhell (1976) its biological racism excludes National Socialism from the family of fascisms. As a result, he argues that it must be treated as *sui generis*, as unclassifiable, a position endorsed by A. J. Gregor (1999). In the US, meanwhile, another scholar's individual journey towards what was later to become a working consensus on fascism's palingenetic core was nearing completion. In 1980 Stanley Payne entered the fray with two seminal publications (1980a, 1980b). They showed the influence both of his colleague George Mosse and of the sociologist and political scientist Juan Linz, who at the time was also making important contributions to fascist studies (Linz

1976, 1980). Payne offered for the first time a coherent taxonomy of fascism as a distinctive category of the extreme right, drawing both on his wide-ranging study of interwar Europe and on his expertise in the specific role played by Falangist fascism in 1930s Spain (Payne 1961). Crucially, his 'typological description' of the ideological goals of generic fascism stressed its all-embracing revolutionary dynamic as understood by the fascists themselves:

> Creation of a new nationalist authoritarian state based not merely on traditional principles or models; Organization of some new kind of regulated, multiclass, integrated national economic structure, whether called national corporatist, national socialist, or national syndicalist; Goal of empire or a radical change in the nation's relationship with other powers; Specific espousal of an idealist, voluntarist creed, normally involving the attempt to realize a new form of modern, self-determined, secular culture. (Payne 1980a)

Unbeknown to them at the time, all these lone researchers, however isolated within their immediate academic circles in their insistence on fascism's revolutionary, *futural* dynamic, were preparing the ground for the dramatic 'coming of age' of comparative fascist studies in the 1990s as a productive and collaborative sub-discipline of history and politics. At this moment, the empathetic approach to fascism's core nature as an ideology suddenly, and almost mysteriously, moved from the periphery to the centre of comparative studies to the point where, after several decades of professional confusion, it seemed to become common sense even for historians who had previously studiously ignored fascist studies. From then on it was increasingly 'self-evident' for experts to take *at face value* the fascists' oft proclaimed belief that they are charged with a mission to overcome the atomization, decadence and materialism of the modern world by creating a new type of nationalist regime, one rooted in a heroic past but embracing a dynamically transformational future. For example, no less a world expert on the Third Reich than Ian Kershaw was now prepared not only to classify Nazism as a form of fascism but to assert that 'The quest for national rebirth lay, of course, at the heart of all fascist movements' (Kershaw 2004: 247).

This vision had been expressed in millions of words in speeches, posters, pamphlets, newspapers, articles, legislation and literary books during the 1920s and 1930s in many languages, but had been conventionally dismissed as 'propaganda' by Marxists and liberals alike, understood not with what we saw earlier were its original connotations of 'dissemination of the faith' but in the sense of cynical brainwashing in order to achieve a monopoly of power. By the mid-1990s such primary sources, instead of being decoded for their reactionary 'capitalist' or irrational, barbarian subtext, started to be increasingly accepted as testimonies of a new secular faith, the foundation stone of which was a blind belief in the imminent palingenesis of the ultra-nation. It is worth pointing out that the ideological texts engaged with or sampled as documents of this faith were not confined to the speeches of fascist leaders or official propaganda but were produced by a wide range of artists, social commentators, journalists, cultural critics, scientists, campaigners for innovation within fascism and intellectuals.

In the context of the fascist 'faith', it is worth pointing out that, inevitably, a fanatical, unquestioning, zealous commitment to the fascist creed is found only within a minority of the members of a large fascist movement, a minority which is smaller still within a fascist party, and even rarer within an entire regime. Like all socio-political movements, the bigger and more successful they become, the more the original vanguard of zealots, for whom the revolutionary vision is the driving force, are joined by opportunists who lack a sophisticated understanding of the ideology or total commitment to the vision that underpinned it. Once a movement forms a regime, there will be no shortage of fellow travellers and careerists drawn into serving the new regime without deep convictions – a situation superbly explored in the case of Italian Fascism by the film *Il conformista* (1970), of German fascism by *Mephisto* (1981) and of French fascism by *Julien Lacombe* (1974). Many more will be 'survivors' who pay lip service to the new norm and its official view of the world, but who are essentially conforming just to stay alive for the sake of themselves and their loved ones, and whose 'real selves' are forced into 'inner emigration' – a pragmatic approach evoked in a famous scene between an idealistic American soldier and a cynical Italian in the anti-war film *Catch 22* (1970).

Significantly, the initials of the Fascist Party stamped on the membership card, PNF, were turned into the acronym *Per necessità familiare* ('out of family necessity'), and those who rushed to join the NSDAP after Hitler's victory were known contemptuously by those who joined before 1933 as *Märzgefallene*, 'those who fell in March', an ironic allusion to a famous statue to the victims of the 1848 revolutions in Vienna and Berlin. References to 'believers' in analyses of fascism apply only to the hard core of the ideologically committed, which would be true of the reconstruction of the beliefs shaping any other ideology, political or religious, since they are necessarily based on the testimonies of the most zealous, idealistic and passionate, not the most apathetic, cynical and calculating.

The establishment of the new paradigm

With hindsight, it can be seen that my own contribution to fascist studies, *The Nature of Fascism*, a sustained attempt to interpret fascism's definitional features and history in terms of an ideal-typical faith in national rebirth, came out at the right time to have some impact, and that it was itself a symptom of the new direction in comparative fascist studies that was 'in the air'. Even ten years earlier the book would probably have sunk without trace. However, published in 1991, it was able to articulate and crystallize the new wave of at least partial agreement on the most effective approach to fascist studies and the ideological core that this approach highlighted. (For a time, I referred to the resulting convergence of expert opinion, somewhat provocatively, as 'the new consensus' (Griffin 1998, 2012a), a phrase which was never meant to imply either total unanimity among scholars or that the growing consensus was with *my own* formulation of the theory.)

Over the next few years, more books and articles consistent with the pioneering efforts of Weber, Mosse, Payne, Gentile and Sternhell, though rarely citing them, were appearing which offered definitions of the sort mentioned earlier alluding to fascism's palingenetic core myth. Fittingly, it was in fascist studies that the transformation first manifested itself comprehensively. An examination of the flurry of anglophone monographs and articles published on Mussolini's regime during the next two decades will show that, in almost every case, its basic ideology and policies are characterized 'empathetically' in terms of the fascists' self-appointed task to create a new type of modern state, whether in the area of political ritual (Gentile 1996; Berezin 1997), cultural policy (Stone 1998), painting (Affron and Antliff 1998; Braun 2000), imperialism (Kallis 2000), modernity (Ben-Ghiat 2001; Gentile 2003), the welfare state (Quine 2002), technology (Schnapp 2004), cinema (Ricci 2008) or racial policy (Cassata 2008).

Christopher Duggan was a long-time member of an inner circle of British historians seemingly intent not only on ridiculing the claim of comparative fascist studies to be a serious and coherent sub-discipline but on discrediting Emilio Gentile's thesis that a mainstay of Fascism was the elaborate political religion it created, which was integral to its sustained bid to bring about not just a political but a cultural, anthropological and temporal revolution in Italy. So, when he used primary sources to document key themes of the everyday, 'intimate' history of Mussolini's under such headings as 'Purifying the Nation's Soul', 'Imparting Faith' and 'Defence of the Race' (Duggan 2012), there could be no doubt a velvet revolution had taken place in Fascist studies and that the empathetic and, hence, 'culturalist' approach was finally becoming mainstream.

As for Nazi studies, a sign of the times was that two major British historians of the Third Reich who had always steered clear of reference to or entanglement in the debate over generic fascism appeared spontaneously prepared to express themselves in the discourse of the palingenetic paradigm. Chapter 9 of Ian Kershaw's biography of Hitler, 'Breakthrough', which deals with the sudden surge in the attraction of his message to the German electorate after the Wall Street Crash, is replete with references to the prospect of rebirth, a new beginning, a new start which now inspired a fanatical following (Kershaw 1998: 313–76). Richard Evans later devoted a chapter of his study of the 'coming of the Third Reich' to 'Hitler's Cultural Revolution' (Evans 2004: 361–460), a phrase which would certainly have seemed self-evident to George Mosse, but which must have been jarring to an earlier generation of historians convinced of Nazism's moral nihilism and 'anti-ideology'.

Since the mid-2000s the recognition of fascism's palingenetic dynamic, whether or not it is expressed in these precise terms, has become second nature to most researchers investigating 'putative' fascism (i.e. political phenomena whose fascist credentials have yet to be established) in interwar Europe, whether in Germany (Esposito 2015b), Italy (Maulsby 2014), Britain (Gottlieb and Linehan 2004), Portugal (Costa Pinto 2000), Spain (Cobo Romero et al. 2016), Romania (Turda 2008a), Hungary (Szele 2015), Croatia (Yeomans 2013), Norway (Emberland 2015), Sweden (Berggren 2002), Estonia (Kasekamp 2000), Ukraine (Shekhovtsov 2008a) or Russia (Umland 2010), and even in some non-European ones, such as Japan (Tansman 2009), South Africa (Beningfield 2006; Marx 2009), Argentina (Ballent 2017) and Brazil (Trajano Filho 2017). There is now a real prospect that interwar fascism will come to be seen not as the arch-enemy of modernism but as the would-be architect of a totalizing modernist culture and state retaining its roots in a mythicized past (Griffin 2008).

Some advice about applying the empathetic paradigm

In offering the following advice to readers who have been persuaded by the argument so far to apply the empathetic approach to fascist ideology, with its emphasis on the revolutionary aspirations at the core of its destructive onslaught on liberal and communist civilization, the intention is to dispel some common misunderstandings so as to ensure its use is an effective heuristic device in essays or research. This is particularly necessary since those unimpressed by this interpretive strategy and the premises that underlie it – the Weberian principle of 'utopian abstraction' in formulating definitions,

Sorelian insights into the mythic drivers of ideologies, and a Mossean emphasis on methodological empathy – cannot be simply ignored. They include not just the many sceptics who participated in a sustained forum discussion about fascism's definition hosted by the German journal *Erwägen Wissen Ethik* in 2006 (Griffin et al. 2014) but also such eminent scholars as Kevin Passmore (2002), James Gregor (2006) and Richard Bosworth (2009). In chapter 6 contemporary calls for a shift in focus in the study of fascism so that neglected aspects of its tangled history can be addressed will be considered directly, but for the moment it is enough to draw attention to a few caveats to help avoid an excessively simplistic or 'Griffino-centric' approach.

The first point to emphasize is that the narrative structure used here to summarize the debate about fascism is inevitably far from neutral. Marxists may well object to their approaches being presented in the first chapter, only to see them implicitly rejected as inadequate, and certainly many of those then categorized as incoherent or confused liberal academics would take issue with my picture of the conceptual chaos in which they participated, and especially the special pleading for a 'third approach' which follows on from this in chapter 2. By dedicating a whole chapter to the 'empathetic paradigm' of fascism, I make no secret of my own professional and emotional stake in presenting it as convincingly as possible and in highlighting the particular features of my own version of it. To counter this built-in 'bias', readers are urged to read widely, to retain their critical judgement and, whatever definition they use, to show in their own analysis that they are fully aware of the contested nature of the term 'fascism', the protracted complexity of the debate, and the need to set out their preferred working definition or ideal type as lucidly as possible.

Second, there exists a peculiar tension between analysing generic fascism as an 'ideal type' and the tendency of language to narrate, reify and essentialize it to the point of treating it like a living entity. Fascism does not objectively 'rise', 'spread', 'fall', 'survive the war' and 'reinvent itself' by 'adapting its core vision to new realities'. It is fascists or, rather, complex living individuals who in a compartment of their lives have adopted fascist convictions to the point of acting on them, who collectively internalize, develop, interpret and enact fascist ideas, and who may feel motivated to adapt their political faith to changing socio-political conditions and 'hard facts'. As an ideal type, generic fascism is a construct, an empty conceptual shell, and has no independent or organic life of its own: only human beings, and the movements, organizations, institutions and regimes which they animate, have any sort of 'real' historical existence, though the very act of writing about them can imbue abstract concepts with a ghostly agency of their own. By the same token, it is important that those using this guide for practical purposes bear in mind that, no matter how many concrete features of a specific historical phenomenon or episode within fascist studies are illuminated by a particular theory or seem to 'fit' the approach recommended here, it cannot 'prove' the theory is right; it can only demonstrate its heuristic value.

It is also important that those influenced by this book do not imply in their own analyses that fascism is primarily an ideology. Certainly, it is defined here ideal-typically on the basis of its core ideological features, just as most other generic political concepts are in the human sciences. However, as a historical and contemporary reality, it is how fascist ideology has been translated into actions and events through the medium of texts, propaganda, plans, policies, organizations, institutions and actions that must be of primary interest to the researcher. In this context, fascism's relationship to doctrine is particularly interesting, because it brings out the distinction, on the one hand, between ideology as a semi-articulated 'vision of the world' (or what the Nazis called *Weltanschauung*) demanding radical or revolutionary action (e.g. liberalism, feminism, fascism) and, on the other, ideology as an orthodox doctrine derived from a fully fledged intellectual model of human society and historical change, which is then taken up by movements trying to enact it (e.g. anarchism, Marxism and ecologism).

In his article on the Fascist regime's political and social doctrine, first published in the newly created *Enciclopedia italiana* in 1932, Benito Mussolini is lucid on this point. He states that his movement 'was not the nursling of a doctrine worked out beforehand with detailed elaboration; it was born of the need for action and it was itself from the beginning practical rather than theoretical.' He points out that, in any case, 'the years which preceded the March to Rome [which allowed Fascism to enter government in late 1922] were years of great difficulty, during which the necessity for action did not permit of research or any complete elaboration of doctrine.' He qualifies this statement with an important assertion, which resonates with the earlier stress on fascism as a secular religion of national rebirth: 'Doctrine, beautifully defined and carefully elucidated, with headlines and paragraphs, might be lacking; but there was to take its place something more decisive: Faith.' He continues:

> Every doctrine tends to direct human activity towards a determined objective; but the action of men also reacts upon the doctrine, transforms it, adapts it to new needs, or supersedes it with something else. A doctrine, then, must be no mere exercise in words, but a living act; and thus the value of Fascism lies in the fact that it is veined with pragmatism, but at the same time has a will to exist and a will to power, a firm front in face of the reality of 'violence'. (Mussolini 1933)

Hitler is even more radical in his condemnation of fascism as a 'pure' ideology. In *Mein Kampf* he stresses the point that, though a 'philosophy of life' or 'vision of the world' provides the premise to human existence, nevertheless, in itself, a *Weltanschauung*, 'even if it is a thousand times correct and of the highest benefit to humanity, will always be irrelevant to the practical shaping of a people's life' [the life of the *Volk*]. For this to occur, its principles must 'become the banner of a fighting movement' which must secure 'the victory of its ideas' so that 'party dogmas' become 'the new state principles of a people's community, the *Volksgemeinschaft*' (Hitler [1926] 1992: 345–6).

Applying the empathetic paradigm to fascist studies should therefore not prioritize theories and definitions but lead to a recognition of fascism's importance to its believers, at least in the interwar period, as a vast sequence of 'living acts' carried out by a 'fighting movement' determined to bring about the palingenesis of the ultra-nation. These are to be carefully reconstructed and analysed through historical and political investigation, without treating the conceptual framework as objectively true or uncontested or as of primary interest. Nor should fascism ever be treated as a static phenomenon. On the contrary, the history of fascism is one of evolving complexity and the pragmatic adaption of basic principles, goals and ideological formulae to constantly changing circumstances which are unique to each country and region, but always with a drive towards revolutionary activism and change.

A final piece of advice is to bear in mind one of Bertolt Brecht's more useful phrases: 'THE TRUTH IS CONCRETE' (he had it written in big letters above his writing desk). It is important that students who have embarked on a project relating to fascism adopt a definition or approach primarily to gain deeper understanding about concrete phenomena, relating where possible to real human beings caught up in the maelstrom of history. Above all, try to end up with topics that interest you and which demand from you considerable individual research and commitment – a principle which, according to Karl Popper, also solves the problem of objectivity in the human sciences (Popper [1957] 2002: 191). Only in this way will you develop a unique grasp of a specialist area of fascist studies illuminated by a consciously adopted theoretical approach, after which excellence will follow and original knowledge will flow forth. By engaging as far as circumstances allow with theories and sources *within the framework of your own independent study and intellectual passions*, you will make any knowledge and interpretation you arrive at your own and (hopefully) discover the true fascination of fascist studies.

4
Interwar Fascism: Permutations of Revolutionary Nationalism

The protean quality of fascist ideology

My own short-hand definition of fascism – first introduced in *The Nature of Fascism* (1991) and reprised in the last chapter as one of many converging and compatible accounts of its main features now available – referred to it as a political ideology whose mythic core of 'palingenetic ultranationalism' remained a constant within 'its various permutations'. This chapter sets out to place some much needed historical flesh on the dry bones of such an abstract formula by showing how even a small sample of the permutations which arose between 1919 and 1945 illustrates the remarkable variety of the species of fascism generated by the same definitional 'minimum' or 'ineliminable' core identified by the empathetic ideal type.

The varying conditions of economic crisis and political instability experienced by so many very different states in Western and partially Westernized areas of the world (Europe, North and South America, South Africa, Japan) during the interwar period caused revolutionary nationalism to assume a wide range of nuanced forms adapted to local conditions. The differentiation of species of the new political genus (known in evolutionary theory as 'speciation') was also encouraged by the nebulousness of the two components of its hybrid core myth referred to in chapter 3, namely the organic 'ultra-nation' and its rebirth. Speciation was also intensified by the fact that – in contrast to Marxist revolutionary theory, which remains recognizably homogeneous despite forming different national dialects – each fascist national myth (or cluster of myths) is an exclusive product of different national strands of interwoven history, culture and collective fantasy, sometimes lived out through the medium of a unique national language. The result of these factors is that, as both an ideology and a political myth, fascism has a pronounced tendency to take on various guises, to be 'polymorphic'. Once it had established a sufficient base as a populist movement in the chaotic 1920s and 1930s to operate on history as a movement (and, in just three instances, as a largely autonomous regime), it spawned a remarkable diversity of specific political, social and cultural visions and policies sometimes *even within the same party*, and proved prone to extensive entanglement with non-fascist phenomena in its struggle for power.

The protean quality of fascism's core myth also helps explain the intensified diversification which the fascist genus underwent after the war, when those who espoused it despite the defeat of the Axis powers had to adapt to a radically new historical environment intensely hostile to revolutionary nationalist projects. They thus generally had to find alternatives to the combination of uniformed paramilitary force and populist movement with a political party to form the 'militia-party' that had been so successfully pioneered by Italian Fascism since 1925 (Gentile 2003: 1).

It is worth stressing that, to illustrate this feature of fascism, this chapter has no intention of producing a sort of *catalogue raisonné* of all its main interwar manifestations, let alone of providing potted histories for them, which in any case has been done admirably elsewhere (e.g. Carsten 1967; Payne 1995; Morgan 2003; Blinkhorn 2000). Nor will it offer a 'master narrative' of a single anthropomorphized entity called 'fascism' in which the author has usually subliminally amalgamated elements taken from both Fascism and Nazism. The specious 'it' that results can then be portrayed as embarking on a perilous journey from its modest beginnings in Milan immediately after the First

World War to a period of apparently irresistible triumph from the late 1930s to the autumn of 1941, only gradually to succumb to catastrophic defeat at the hands of the Allies in 1945. One effect of such a misleadingly simplistic narrative approach is that the host of highly original fascist movements that never gained autonomous state power in the 1930s and 1940s tend to be ignored, or dismissed as peripheral to its paradigmatic manifestation in the European Axis powers (Fascist Italy and Nazi Germany), with little to reveal about the genus as a whole. Despite the tendency of language to reify and anthropomorphize, fascism is an even more stubbornly plural, polymorphic political entity than socialism, liberalism, feudalism and many other political 'isms'. As a result, it makes sense to treat each movement 'equally' as far as understanding the genus is concerned, though not, of course, in terms of its historical consequences. This means approaching every manifestation of fascism as yet another unique permutation of revolutionary ultranationalism shaped by local factors, and hence as a potentially important source of fresh insights into fascism's nature as a political actor and social force, whether it failed in its bid to conquer state power or not (Griffin 2015a).

An immediate result of this approach is that neither Fascism nor National Socialism is 'privileged' here as the revelation of the essence of fascism, its logical endpoint or its paradigm as an ideology. This is not to deny that, first, Fascism in the 1920s, and then Nazism in the 1930s, exerted a major influence as a role model for indigenous fascist movements in many Europeanized countries. But in the present context the two movements are approached simply as particular variants of fascism, the first characterized by the attempt to modernize Italy mainly through activating the myth of its Roman heritage, the second by its radically biologized and scientized racism, by enormously ambitious imperialist goals, and by its readiness to enforce through repression and terror a radical and ruthless process of creative destruction in every sphere which had no parallel in Fascist Italy. In short, each fascism is understood here *both* as typical of the wider political genus and as idiosyncratic, and studied with an eye *both* for its unique aspects – which particularly interest historians working 'idiographically' – and for its generic ones – of particular concern to political scientists working 'nomotheti-cally' (Levy 2012).

This principle can be illustrated using the example of the Third Reich. Certainly, it was the unique or exceptional aspects of Nazism that enabled it to play such a devastating role in modern history once it became the legal basis of a regime. Before Hitler came to power, Germany was already a highly modernized and industrialized nation with a powerful state apparatus, an advanced civil society and an intensely patriotic population. It thus lent itself to being transformed into a powerful totalitarian regime once its 'late' democratic nation-state, the Weimar Republic, entered a sustained crisis. Compared with Italian Fascism and all other fascisms in less developed countries, Nazism was thus endowed with a unique capacity for committing crimes against humanity on an industrial scale. Nevertheless, it was able to penetrate the weakened protective membrane of a failing liberal democracy only in the exceptional circumstances created by the extreme conditions following the Wall Street Crash. Thanks to the collusion of political and social elites who feared chaos and the threat of the left more than they feared totalitarianism, the Nazis were allowed to enter the citadel of state power in 1933, with catastrophic consequences.

Despite all these exceptional circumstances, even the most cursory study of the core myth driving the Nazis' attempted totalitarian revolution indicates that it is one of the imminent rebirth of the nation-race from decadence, a palingenetic vision that shaped and structured the regime's entire assault on the Weimar system and the many categories of human beings, ideologies and institutions that Nazism identified as the enemies of, or obstacles to, rebirth. In this sense, even Nazism, despite the unparalleled scale of its atrocities, is to be regarded as simultaneously unique *and* the manifestation of generic fascism, and *no more so than any other species of the genus*.

This approach, stressing both the unique and the generic as two aspects of a Janus-headed fascist politics, will now be applied to a small selection of topics encountered in the comparative study of fascism – the 'ultra-nation', the foundation myth, gender politics, modernism and economics – with reference to just a few of the many movements that arose in the interwar period. What follows is inevitably superficial and incomplete. It can do no more than provide an impression of how nuanced the historical texture of individual interwar fascisms were despite belonging to the same political genus. As Fascist Italy and Nazi Germany provide the only example of fascist regimes established in peacetime, it seems appropriate to start by comparing their conception of the ultra-nation that was to arise phoenix-like after the 'decadent' age of liberal democracy and communism had been ended.

The fascist ultra-nation

While the concept of the organic national community under-going a process of rebirth is *by (ideal-typical) definition* a common denominator of all fascisms, it soon becomes clear when individual fascist ultranationalist myths are examined in the 'fascist era' (1918–45) that there is a wide spectrum of possibilities in the way that organism can be conceived. Furthermore, a single movement may host varied, and sometimes conflicting, currents of national and racial thinking if it grows to a point where it is joined by significant sections of the educated classes, who naturally represent many professions, world-views and disciplines, all with their own imaginings of the nation or race, diagnoses of its decadence, and prescriptions for the remedies needed to bring about its rebirth. What David Roberts observes about ideology in Mussolini's regime could be applied to all fascist movements: it was, in stark contrast to the image of perfect organization, homogeneity and cohesion presented in propaganda, a 'messy mixture' (Roberts 2000: 208). The extreme heterogeneity of fascist organic nationalism can be illustrated by comparing the conflicting ways the ultra-nation was visualized in Fascist Italy and Nazi Germany.

The mythicized Italy at the heart of the project of rebirth pursued by Italian Fascism was a kaleidoscopic composite of various imaginings of the nation: the monarchical Italy identified with the House of Savoy now entering a golden age; the united nation-state born of the Risorgimento which was now being completed by Mussolini's regime; the Mazzinian Italy of the 'people' finally realized by the *duce*; the heroic Italy of the Alpine trenches facing the Austrians in the First World War now determining the ethos of the new regime; the 'Great Power' that would finally have its own African Empire emulating the Roman past; the historic Italy of the city-states, of Dante, of Renaissance art now inspiring a new Italian culture; the proto-Italy which gave the world the Catholic Church and was now ushering in a new civilization; the rural Italy of *strapaese* ('hyper-countryside'), with its glorious agricultural lushness, majestic mountains, rolling hills, vineyards, seascapes, regional cultures, medieval hill-top towns and local traditions which would be honoured under Mussolini. Yet at the same time the reborn nation embraced the futurist Italy of *stracittà* ('hyper-city') urbanization, with its technological progress, futuristic transport systems, aviation, radio communication, transatlantic travel, athletics and spectator sports, modernist art and architecture, new towns, a new type of corporatist economy, a welfare state, and powerful armed forces equipped with the latest military technology.

There were also from the outset of the regime more sinister currents feeding the myth of the nation: a natalist campaign concerned with boosting Italy's demographic growth and racial health (Quine 2012); strands of anti-Semitism some from within the Catholic Church itself (Ben-Ghiat 2001: 148–56); and a home-grown tradition of eugenics and racial theory (Cassata 2011). This largely ignored racist undercurrent, which refutes disingenuous assumptions that Fascist racism was a late and highly un-Italian import from Nazi Germany, ensured a plentiful supply of 'racial experts' prepared to draft anti-miscegenation laws in 1937 to protect the Italian race (*gente, stirpe, razza*) from contamination by African blood and to formulate the infamous anti-Semitic race laws of 1938. These invoked the scientific 'fact' of the Aryan origins of the Italians, despite Mussolini mocking the Nazi fixation with the purity of their race a few years earlier.

As we shall see shortly, a key mythic component of every fascist ultranationalism is a foundation myth of its origins, which may well predate its development into a nation-state. The dominant foundation myth of Fascism was the vision of modern Italians as direct descendants from and spiritual heirs of the Romans. This heritage was conceived not in genetic terms of purity of blood (which would have been a nonsense given the multi-ethnic nature of the Roman Empire) but as the animating force of a generation whose rediscovery of their Roman identity would inspire them to bring about a renaissance of greatness, as much cultural, technological and social as imperial and military, thereby turning Italy into a 'Third Rome' (Kallis 2014), a counter-myth to the 'Third Reich'. It was thus Italy's 'Romanness', *romanità*, that became the template for so much of Fascism's political religion, public works, style of the *duce* cult, foreign policy, aesthetic and architecture, and that inspired the vast EUR exhibition in Rome planned to present Fascist Italy as inaugurating a new phase of world civilization, as the Roman Empire had done over two millennia earlier (Nelis 2007; Kallis 2014).

But Fascist myth was polymorphic and dynamic, and *romanità* was only one current shaping the vision of the Fascist New Man and New Woman who would inhabit the New Italy (Dagnino 2016). Over time the Fascist utopia shifted significantly from the leftist anti-clericalism and republicanism of the earliest 'San Sepolcro' Fascism to an ideology that embraced the Vatican and the monarchy, before entering an imperialist and then militaristic phase (1933–43), and then changing once again after the armistice of 1943. In its last incarnation, as the Italian Social Republic and a puppet regime of the Third Reich, Fascism, now resolutely anti-clerical and anti-monarchical, became the official ally of Nazism in the creation of a European New Order to be defended from destruction by the US, the USSR and world Jewry, thus providing a final theatrical projection of the 'new Italy', its mythic roots transferred from a Roman to an Aryan soil.

The Nazi ultra-nation

Even this highly condensed summary of currents within Fascist political culture underlines how facile it is to contrast too starkly its 'cultural' – and therefore by implication relatively harmless – ultranationalism with the Nazis' 'biological racism'. Certainly, the foundation myth that Germans were descended from an Aryan super-race (Poliakov 1974) ensured that Nazism absorbed a far more poisonous dose of scientized racism into official culture than did Italian Fascism. This corruption of nationalism was made easier by the fact that, in contrast to Italy, for over a century German academic and intellectual life had offered a hospitable environment for a number of toxic theories, including positive and negative eugenics, ancestral and heredity studies, social hygiene, racial anthropology, racial geopolitics and polygenesis (which denied a common origin and level of humanness to all ethnic groups). Under Weimar, 'racial science' was given both a central organization and an enhanced legitimacy with the foundation in 1927 of the Kaiser Wilhelm Institute of Anthropology, Human Heredity, and Eugenics, an institution which collaborated in the creation of the world's first science-based racial state (Burleigh and Wippermann 1991; Weiss-Wendt and Yeomans 2013).

Yet Nazi ultranationalism was also extremely variegated, with a strong contribution from the hyperpatriotism inherited from the Second Reich and the First World War, powerful traditions of cultural ultranationalism which stretched the German imagined community to embrace the glories of its medieval cathedrals, Baroque music, Romantic literature and painting, modern imperialism, colonialism and militaristic chauvinism, as well as celebrations of German industry, technology and the qualities of the national character that had nothing specifically biological about them. One of the most important influences on Nazi nationalism was the nineteenth-century *völkisch* movement, which was itself highly heterogeneous, embracing occultist (Goodrick-Clarke 2004), pagan, 'blood and soil', colonial, Romantic and pseudo-Christian currents, and only in some instances overlapped with 'scientific' racism (Mosse 1975). The result is that Nazism never developed a coherent ultranationalism any more than Fascism did. Rather, it established a composite, dynamically shifting and flexible one in which both 'racial science' and *völkisch* nationalism were formed of conflicting currents, and key concepts such as the Nordic, the Germanic, 'blood', *Volk* and *Art* (the healthy German racial 'genus') remained as much metaphors for mythic spiritual qualities of the heroic national character as material categories of racial purity (Weiss-Wendt and Yeomans 2013).

Whether it was rationalized pseudo-scientifically or through *völkisch* fantasy, it is the obsession with the Germans' racial purity that marks the deepest contrast with Fascist ultranationalism. The promulgation of race laws in 1938 asserting the Aryan ancestry of the Italians and the exclusion of Jews from the Italian national community contradicted the foundation myth of Fascism, which asserted the Italians' ancestry in a multi-ethnic, multicultural and multi-faith Roman Empire, and certainly went against the grain of ordinary Italians, who remained unreceptive to the 'racist turn' in Fascist propaganda. By contrast, the Nuremberg Race Laws of 1935 were *consistent* with fantasies of the Aryan heritage which had been disseminated and refined in Germany ever since the mid-nineteenth century and enjoyed substantial populist backing. As a result, while Fascism focused for much of its life on 'nationalizing' Italians in a totalitarian spirit which did not extend to a terror apparatus, Nazism set about 'Aryanizing' and 'Nordifying' Germans, using all-pervasive state propaganda, racial legislation, a thoroughly Nazified educational system and academia, both the humanities and (wherever possible) the natural sciences, and organizations of mass social engineering, including an extensive terror apparatus and an all-pervasive censorship regime, as well as institutional bodies and associations of all kinds, to promote and enforce a blend of biological, patriotic and *völkisch* strands of racial consciousness. 'Aryanization' and 'Nordification' also penetrated deep into the aesthetics of ritual Nazi theatre (Niven 2000), the many experiments in creating 'German' painting, sculpture and architecture (Adam 1992), and even the Newspeak of the citizens of the Reich (Klemperer 2006). In Leni Riefenstahl's documentary of the 1936 Berlin Olympics, *Olympia* (1938), German athletes morph into Classical Greek sporting heroes to produce graphic images (at least for believers) of the anthropological revolution that was taking place in the Third Reich. Similarly, the austere Graeco-Roman style of Nazi civic architecture can be seen as symbolizing not nostalgia for the past but the rebirth of the Aryan spirit by evoking an 'eternal' aesthetic (Griffin 2017). Here, as in so much of Nazi culture, there was a fusion of aesthetics and eugenics (Maertz 2017).

It should be clear from the above that what linked the most dedicated Fascists and Nazis was the fact that both pursued fascist programmes of national rebirth, but that what separated them was their commitment to very different combinations of ultranationalist myth. As a result, even apparently common elements may conceal deep divides. For example, idealized neo-Classical sculptures of naked male athletes in sporting venues are a feature of both the Fascist and Nazi regimes. Yet it would be deeply mistaken to assume that both embody the same aesthetic or the same vision of national renewal. The convinced Fascist saw in such works the Classical ideal of the human form to be emulated by modern Romans in Mussolini's Third Rome. The dedicated Nazi recognized in them a eugenic ideal, an archetype of the eternal Aryan, a member of a biological super-race whose closest and 'purest' living ancestors in the modern world were the Germans, and which would live again in a Third Reich now being purged of every manifestation of the degenerate and the dysgenic. Such a comparison highlights the value of comparing foundation myths as a short-cut to recognizing the uniqueness of each permutation of fascism's palingenetic ideology of the ultra-nation's rebirth.

The variety of fascism's foundation myths

Both Fascism and Nazism arose in countries which achieved unification only in the nineteenth century. The invocation of a primordial imperial past (Fascism) or a racial wellspring of cultural creativity and heroism lost in the mists of time (Nazism) enabled a fascist regime to conjure up a mythic narrative of palingenesis envisioned as the renewal of an ancient period of greatness, an explosion of collective cultural creativity after a sustained interval of historical insignificance or decay in which there had been no state to contain and channel the hereditary energies of the national community. This pattern of past greatness, decay and renewal proves adaptable to a wide diversity of historical and cultural contexts in which the fascist myth is to be forged.

Romanian fascism (known both as the Legion of the Archangel Michael and the Iron Guard), which twice shared state power before being finally crushed, illustrates just how original, but also how elaborate, other fascist foundation myths and fantasies of national renewal could become in interwar Europe. Romania had extricated itself from the Ottoman Empire only in modern times, and its territory was vastly expanded as a result of the First World War, with Hungarians, Germans, Jews, Bulgarians and Ukrainians together making up nearly a third of citizens by the 1920s. To invent the Romanian ultra-nation, the intellectuals of the Legion of the Archangel Michael had recourse to their own brand of 'ethnogenetic' historical speculation about the origins of their people (Bucur 2002; Turda 2015). However, they combined it not with the eugenic speculation that was rife in Romania but with elements appropriated from Eastern European proto-anthropology and from the eschatological traditions of the Romanian Orthodox Church concerning the end of human history. As a result, a proud, heroic, organic people, the Dacians, homogeneous both ethnically and spiritually, was born in the palingenetic imagination of the Legionaries, who saw its descendants (by now largely illiterate peasants) charged with a unique mission in the modern age, namely to purge the nation of decadence, create the *omul nou* (the New Man) and achieve collective 'resurrection'.

Much of the Legion's fantasy of the heroic ancestry of modern Romanians centred on the formative role in the birth of the nation played by one particular group of tribes, the ancient Geto-Dacians. These were an Iron Age people supposedly of Indo-European (Aryan!) ethnicity, located in the area in and around the Carpathian Mountains and west of the Black Sea, and studied by a branch of Thracology known as Dacology. Legionary intellectuals attributed to this tribal people the heroic qualities and cultural resilience that enabled its descendants to avoid total subjugation by the Roman Empire in the second century AD, which allowed it to produce the racial hybrid of Daco-Romans which subsequently developed into the modern Romanians. Meetings of the Iron Guard sometimes opened with a ceremony commemorating Decebal, supposedly the last independent Dacian king (Cinpoes 2016).

This scientistic strand of Romanian fascism was combined incongruously with a powerful pseudo-religious element derived from the identification of Romanian-ness with Christianity, an imaginative leap which itself blended two mythic narratives. Crucial for the Legion's political religion was its incorporation of elements taken from the rituals and iconography of the Romanian Orthodox Church to a point where national rebirth within historical time was conflated with the imagined resurrection of entire nations on the Day of Judgement. This strand was enriched by the identification of the movement with the Archangel Michael, whose legendary powers as a divine dragon-slayer in the mists of time were recoded within Legionary iconography to symbolize implicitly a ruthless existential war against the many alleged enemies of the sacred 'ţara' (fatherland): Jews, Hungarians, Germans, Slavs, Gypsies, the liberal state, the corrupt monarchy, communists, cosmopolitanism and modernity itself. The result was a mystic piety directed towards the reborn nation and its leader, Corneliu Codreanu (sometimes painted as an icon), fused with a martyric death cult (Rusu 2016) in which the death of the Legionary assassins and their victims was sacralized.

The preoccupation of Romanian ultranationalists with their purported Dacian ancestry is technically termed 'protochronism' (from the Greek for 'earliest time') (Turda 2008b), and several other fascist ultranationalisms are based on a protochronist myth in the absence of a more tangible medieval or early modern Golden Age to invoke as the basis of a rebirth. For example, Ustasha's vision of a Croatian ultra-nation locked in a struggle for survival against a range of ethnic and ideological enemies originated, like so many of Europe's 'invented traditions' of nationhood, can be traced to the rise of nineteenth-century wishful thinking about a distinctive Yugoslav or Balkan people, speculation that also lent itself to being cloaked in the scientistic discourse of physical and cultural proto-anthropology. Some currents of nationalist academic confabulation postulated an idealized Serbian genotype as the decisive component of a common Yugoslav Dinaric identity. Inevitably, this thesis was soon countered by the claim of Croatian nationalists that Dinaric Croatians were distinct from and racially *superior* to Serbs, who were not even Dinaric (Bartulin 2013). During the Second World War, such academic fictions of racial distinctiveness would have lethal consequences in the concentration camps of Ustasha.

Meanwhile, in Hungary, the ideologues of the Arrow Cross were able to draw on over a decade of extensively academic speculation, also rooted in the rise of scientized nationalism in the nineteenth century, about the ethnic origin and unique national character of a purported Magyar root race (Turda and Gillette 2014). While in the 1930s Nazi racial experts were refining Aryan science, legislation and the apparatus of repression against non-Aryans, in contemporary Hungary anthropologists, racial experts, philologists and eugenicists of a nationalist persuasion set about creating their own ultra-nation. Soon evidence was being accumulated for the descent of contemporary Hungarians from a non-Aryan, non-Indo-European warrior root race blending Finno-Ugric with Turkic and Mongol elements (the precise composition varied according to the theorist). When members of the Arrow Cross cooperated with Nazis to exterminate over 450,000 Hungarian Jews in the summer of 1944, they did so on the basis of equivalent but diametrically opposed myths of racial purity and superiority (Szele 2015), both of which identified a host of common enemies to be purged.

Protochronic myth also played a key role in the imagined nation of Scandinavian fascisms. Inevitably, the heroized myth of their Viking ancestry played a role in the ultranationalism of the Norwegian Nasjonal Samling, which used runes and allusions to Norse myths and imagery in its construction of the Norwegians as a primordial heroic race. The Norse variant of the fascist foundation myth is still central to the contemporary international Odinist strand of neo-fascism (Kaplan 1997: 69–99). The same need for mythic roots is evident in the formation of the Finnish Patriotic People's Movement (IKL), founded in 1932 as a continuation of the ultranationalist Lapuan movement after it was banned. In contrast to Ustasha and the Arrow Cross, the IKL sense of primordial identity was free of biological racism, though not of anti-Semitism or irredentist longings for a 'Greater Finland'. Its sense of Finnish uniqueness was based on radical linguistic and cultural divisions from Swedes and Russians, as well as on the enduring impact of 'Karelianism', a form of Romantic nationalism reminiscent of the Celtic Revival and the German *völkisch* movement in art and literature, but which saw in the national epic *The Kalevala* the embodiment of a uniquely Finnish national character and vision of the world, now being incorporated within a modern ultra-nation (Karvonen 1988).

Protochronic speculation as the basis of palingenetic fantasy was rendered superfluous if the past could deliver a 'Golden Age' within recorded time to be revived in a total cultural renewal. In Spain, the *siglo de oro* (1492–1659), with its monarchical absolutism, imperial power, the authority of the Church and outstanding artistic achievements, became the role model for the cultural and political renaissance that the Falangist art critic Ernesto Caballero strove to bring about under General Franco (Wahnón 2017). Similarly, the British Union of Fascists looked for inspiration for a Greater Britain to the glories of the Elizabethan age, when art, poetry, theatre and music flowered, imperial and naval power expanded, and English science and technology dominated the world (Gottlieb and Linehan 2004). Likewise, the National Socialist Movement in Holland (NSB) invoked the Dutch Golden Age of the seventeenth century, when, having liberated itself from the Spanish yoke, the country's trade, science, military and imperial strength, and art were among the most prestigious in the world. Meanwhile, French fascists (and Vichy's para-fascist regime) revisited the liberal myth of the overthrow of the monarchy and devised an anti-republican, authoritarian 'National Revolution' which rationalized its collaborationist, anti-Semitic agenda (Arnold 2000: 133–92). In South Africa, the Ossewabrandwag (Ox-wagon Sentinel) identified the struggle of the Boers to create a viable colony before the British occupation as the evidence that they constituted an organic ultra-nation now experiencing its rebirth (Marx 2009).

One of the most original foundation myths, blending protochronic with Golden Age fantasies, was developed by the Brazilian Integralist Action (AIB). Given the complex racial mixing in a country where indigenous peoples and the descendants of generations of Portuguese colonizers and of their African slaves had intermarried through the centuries, Plínio Salgado could not indulge in any scientistic notions of biological purity, eugenics or a mythic ancestral super-race. Instead, for him, the essence of the Brazilian-ness (*Brasilidade*) that would provide the cohesive spiritual force needed for the country's rebirth lay precisely in its unique ethnic and cultural blend which had made the rise of Brazil as a powerful modern economy and political nation possible. The AIB thus celebrated the very miscegenation so feared by Nazi, Legionary, Hungarist and Ustasha racists (Turda and Gillette 2014).

Until his movement was banned by the dictator Getúlio Vargas in 1938, Salgado campaigned for Brazil to be seen as an ideal laboratory in which to demonstrate the power of a racially mixed society to revitalize a nation spiritually and culturally, and hence politically and economically, and so lay the foundations of the 'fourth era of humanity' (Bottura 2009). With Salgado safely exiled to Portugal, Vargas was happy to promote the AIB's conciliatory myth of racial blending under his own regime.

The variety of fascist gender politics

The patriarchal assumptions of fascism in the sphere of gender politics have been well documented. Under both Fascism and Nazism, the female body (and ultimately the male too) belonged to the state and had to serve the national community (Horn 1994; Stephenson 2001). Both regimes claimed that, by returning them to their 'natural' biological roles of mothers and homemakers, they had liberated women from their 'false' emancipation by feminism, which according to Fascist propaganda was responsible for the sterility and hysteria of 'the crisis woman' (*donna crisi*), who had escaped the thrall of domesticity only to live out a trivial, vain, narcissistic existence which denatured her gender.

But more recent research has revealed a greater degree of spontaneous collusion with and support for fascism by women's organizations and individual activists than simplistic preconceptions about patriarchy would anticipate (Passmore 2003). Particularly erroneous is the notion that fascism simply wanted to return women to the roles envisaged for them by traditional conservatives. Certainly, once married, women were encouraged to increase the birth rate by a combination of sustained propaganda idealizing motherhood (in Italy with echoes of the cult of the Madonna), financial incentives for taking married women out of the workplace, and medals for large families. But fascist natalism under the *duce* and the *Führer* exhibited a distinctively modernizing and anti-conservative element. The innovations introduced to improve the demographic health of the nation, such as state investment in maternity assistance and infant medicine, anticipated aspects of female healthcare familiar in modern democratic welfare states, but without the liberal emphasis on individualism or the rights of the woman (Quine 2002).

Moreover, women were now encouraged to re-experience their commitment to family life, domesticity and motherhood within the context of an official world-view that attributed a heroic role to their self-sacrifice for the sake of the future generations, a myth that proved attractively empowering to a minority of women searching for greater agency in both Fascist Italy (De Grazia 1992) and Germany (Pine 1997), and even to some former suffragettes in England (Gottlieb 2000). Consistent with this redefinition of gender roles, which encouraged women to experience themselves as full members of the national community, both regimes incited women in their youth and adulthood to join mass organizations intended to socialize them into the activist fascist mentality at work and play, as well as increasing their physical strength and work ethic. This meant that, for millions of females in Germany, and especially in Italy, women's first real experience of modernity was taking part in uniformed paramilitary activities in a youth organization, in auxiliary work for the armed forces, or in communal (but ununiformed) free time activities organized by the national Dopolavoro (After Work) or Kraft durch Freude (Strength through Joy) leisure organizations.

But important national differences in fascist gender politics are not hard to find. The deeply Catholic social environment of Fascism and Falangism ensured that, in contrast to Nazism, there was no question in Italy or Spain of endorsing either the negative eugenics that in the Third Reich led to the sterilization or liquidation of women considered physically or mentally defective or the categorization of millions of women in occupied Eastern Europe and Russia as specimens of a subhuman, racially inferior branch of humanity who could be allowed to survive only as slaves of the regime. Under Mussolini or Franco, there could be no question of women undergoing the equivalent of the so-called Mischling Test (test of racial mixing) that their German counterparts had to take before marriage to establish the Aryanness of their blood. Nor would there have been any attempt in a (post-) Catholic country to emulate the Nazi *Lebensborn* (Wellspring of Life) initiative to mass-produce healthy babies from good Aryan parentage, which involved setting up human stud farms where SS officers could pass on their genetic qualities.

Under the wartime Ustasha state, gender politics were further nuanced. The influence of theories taken from Eastern European currents of eugenics, racial hygiene and pro-natalist demographic theory combined with prevalent Catholic assumptions to create a sustained 'doublethink' on racial questions. Croatian women were encouraged to return to domesticity and fulfil their 'natural' function as home-makers, reproducers and moral guardians of the race. Catholic morality, reinforced by the conspicuous support of some Catholic clergy for the regime, also denied women abortion and precluded Ustasha from applying negative eugenics to prevent Croatian women deemed racially unhealthy from breeding, just as it protected Croatians with a hereditary disease from a Nazi-style euthanasia campaign. Yet, in contrast to Fascist Italy, Ustasha's militia had no equivalent scruples about determining the fate of their 'enemies' on secular racial grounds (Yeomans 2002). As a result, the Ustasha concentration camps became enclosed killing fields to 'cleanse' Croatia of Serbs, Jews and Gypsies, female and male, on a scale which, in terms of the percentage of the population killed, was the equivalent of the Final Solution in Europe. The biggest camp, Jasenovac, alone accounted for over 80,000 murders committed in individual acts of brutality without the anonymity of gas chamber mass killings.

Clearly, had more fascisms come to power, each regime would have developed its own permutation of ultranationalist gender politics. Judging by their ideology, only a minority would have officially identified categories of women to be sterilized or murdered, and some may have encouraged the emancipation of women within the limits of a fascist state by promoting active service to the nation even after marriage. One can only speculate how many fascist movements, once reduced to collaborationist puppets of the Third Reich, would have in practice colluded with the Nazis' eliminationist policies towards its alleged racial and genetic enemies, female as well as male, as part of the New European Order.

The variety of fascist modernism

The degree to which each fascism embraced or rejected the aesthetics of cultural modernism in its conventional art-historical sense was again highly variegated. In contrast to the Third Reich, where Goebbels's Reich Chamber of Culture imposed a draconian censorship in every sphere of cultural production, Fascism had an inefficient propaganda apparatus and imposed no official regime style or aesthetic censorship. Instead, it operated on the principle of a 'hegemonic pluralism' that welcomed all artistic creativity as long as it was dedicated to or associated with the rebirth of Italy made possible by the providential leadership of the *duce* (Stone 1998).

As a result, important modernist talents, such as Filippo Marinetti, Umberto Boccioni, Giuseppe Terragni, Adalberto Libera and Mario Sironi, were just some of thousands of highly creative Italians who freely contributed to an extraordinary outpouring of contemporary painting, sculpture, design, photography, fashion, cinema, public art, architecture and town planning, including entire new towns, not to mention a profusion of avant-garde art, design and fine art journals, and important cultural projects such as the *Enciclopedia italiana* (which contained many contributions by non-Fascists). In doing so, they indirectly conferred legitimacy on a regime which boasted that, as part of the all-pervasive process of renewal, it was inaugurating a cultural and intellectual renaissance as yet another expression of Italy's eternal genius.

This mood of renewed national creativity was proactively stimulated through a steady flow of competitions, exhibitions and visionary public works, such as the new system of *autostrada*, or Cinecittà, Italy's own Hollywood. In its fusion of Roman Classicism with the 'stripped' neo-Classicism of 1930s New Objectivity, Rome's new university, La Sapienza, designed by Marcello Piacentini, embodied Fascism's ideal of 'rooted modernism', one which evoked the heroic values of a glorious past (in this case ancient Rome), while fully embracing modern functionality (Kallis 2014). Fascist 'new towns' such as Sabaudia, built in the 'littorial' style of Fascist modernism on land reclaimed from malaria-infested marshes, embodied the creation of a supposedly autarkic agricultural economy coupled with cutting-edge modern planning, technology, hygiene and demographic policy realized in a 'Roman' spirit of national renewal, and produced images of a balance between the past and the present economically, ideologically and aesthetically which fleetingly captured the Fascist utopia.

In France, a prolific fascist intellectual culture grew up after 1918 with its roots in the *fin-de-siècle* rebellion against decadence. In practice, it rarely progressed beyond the first, proto- or pre-movement stage of utopian ultranationalism, and the one major exception to this, the Croix de Feu, eventually renounced revolution and became a democratic party. Yet it underlines the sheer variety of fascist cultural thought that many within the French ultranationalist intelligentsia, who in the 1930s would become admirers of the Third Reich, expressed even more unequivocal enthusiasm for modernist aesthetics than their Italian counterparts. They saw the ethos of the new France adumbrated not in French neo-Classicism but in the works of such figures as the symbolist painter Maurice Denis, the architects Le Corbusier and Auguste Perret, the sculptors Charles Despiau and Aristide Maillol, the 'New Vision' photographer Germaine Krull and the Fauve Maurice Vlaminck (Antliff 2007).

Even Nazism's relationship with aesthetic modernism is far more ambivalent than is generally understood. For decades, the hostility of the Third Reich to most experimental painting styles, epitomized in the infamous 'Degenerate Art Exhibition', the closing of the Bauhaus (a major force in modernist architecture), the burning of 'decadent' books and the banning of jazz and atonal music, was taken to signify that fascism as a whole was not just anti-modern, but anti-*modernist*. Yet a faction within the Nazi leadership saw (non-communist) German Expressionism as embodying a Faustian spirit which was archetypally Aryan. In 1934 Berlin even hosted an exhibition of Italian *Aeropittura*, a branch of futurism, which was opened with a visionary speech by the arch-Expressionist poet Gottfried Benn. Meanwhile, Goebbels lionized Edvard Munch (the Norwegian painter of *The Scream*) for his expression of the Nordic spirit, and some SS Officers (as well as Goebbels) remained ardent jazz fans despite official censorship. In the visual arts, the international rationalist style of architecture was used for factories, bridges, power stations and even some civic buildings, while the design of the Volkswagen was so advanced that in 2006 it was featured in the Victoria and Albert Museum exhibition 'Modernism: Designing a New World'. Perhaps more surprisingly, in 1933 Hitler himself spoke at a conference on culture of the need for design to exhibit 'a functionalism of crystalline clarity' (Dyckhoff 2002).

Approached from this angle, it becomes clear that the use of stripped neo-Classicism for iconic Nazi civic buildings such as the House of German Art or Tempelhof Airport is to be seen not as anti-modern, but as Nazism's own revolutionary aesthetic, a hybrid of ancient and modern again suggesting a form of the 'rooted modernism' typical of generic fascism (Griffin 2017). Equally, the time-defying ethos of Speer's project for rebuilding Berlin in the 'eternal' spirit of 'Aryan' Classical antiquity can also be understood as modernist in its paradoxically futural thrust towards a national eternity (Michaud 2004).

In short, in the revolutionary political context of interwar fascism, it is important not to approach fascist culture solely through the familiar lens of aesthetic categories provided by the conventional history of art. 'Modernism', once seen in a wider socio-cultural or anthropological perspective, does not refer solely to stylistic experimentation; it also invokes an ethos of embracing the liquid flux of modernity with the life-asserting, future-embracing attitude of what Peter Osborne calls 'affirming the temporality of the new' (Osborne 1995: 142). It is a response to the dynamic, creative-destructive aspect of modern life which was enthusiastically embraced by futurism and resonates with the exhortation of Ezra Pound, a doyen of modernism and major propagandist of Italian Fascism (Feldman 2013), to 'make it new' (Pound 1935). In that sense, Nazism's urge to explode the continuum of history with a radical, totalizing experiment in creating a new socio-political order can be seen as the very incarnation of modernism (Fritzsche 1996). In their different ways, then, both Fascist Italy and Nazi Germany should perhaps be considered 'modernist states' (Griffin 2007), despite their very different cultural styles, regimes of social control and obsessions with mythic pasts.

The variety of fascist economics

In economics, too, there was no single fascist model to be adopted, beyond the assertion that the economy should promote the rebirth of the ultra-nation in the first phase and subsequently sustain its new-found greatness, making attempts to generalize hazardous (Baker 2006). In contrast to Bolshevism, then, the transformation of the capitalist system was not seen as the precondition for delivering the revolution. Instead, as is clear from Leni Riefenstahl's propaganda film *The Triumph of the Will*, officially the main driver of change was to be voluntarism, the revolutionary 'will' of the reborn national community, awakened and orchestrated by the charismatic leader and channelled into heroic activity, creativity, productivity and innovation in every sphere. Naturally, both regimes were drawn towards significant state intervention in the building of an industrial-military complex, the achievement of autarky, and the imposition of a war economy so that their imperialist ambitions could be realized. But, had the Axis powers won the war, it is a matter of speculation what would have happened to European capitalism, though the secret use made of Swiss banks as part of the war effort (Lebor 1997) suggests some sort of hybrid system of totalitarian state control working in tandem with international monetary institutions might have emerged.

There is no doubt that, for the most radical fascists, the longer-term aim was to replace the profound social inequality and atomizing individualism produced by capitalism and class stratification with a national community whose members were protected from exploitation and deprivation by a highly interventionist state managing the economy in the interests of the whole nation, conceived as an ethnically or culturally homogeneous organism. Hence Goebbels's declaration that the Nazis were 'mortal enemies of the present capitalist economic system with its exploitation of whoever is economically weak, with its injustice in wealth distribution', and that the Nazis were determined 'to bring down an old world and create a new one, to destroy to make way for a new creation, right to the last stone' (Pellicani 2012).

Both the palingenetic and genocidal implications of this vision and the primacy of racial politics over economics (Mason [1966] 1972) were spelt out in a speech made by Hitler in 1938:

> The creative bearer of this rebirth is the National Socialist Workers Party ... It had to cleanse Germany of all parasites for whom the distress of the Fatherland and of the people was a source of personal enrichment. It had to recognize the eternal value of blood and soil and raise them to the level of the governing laws of our life. (Hitler 1942: 242)

What this actually meant in practical terms for the economics of the New European Order had the war been won by the Axis powers will never be known. In the meantime, the Third Reich showed itself perfectly prepared to harness the power of independent financial institutions, private industry, big business and the manufacturing sector as long as they served the nation's interests (Tooze 2006).

The Fascists operated in a similarly pragmatic way, mixing laissez-faire capitalism with state planning, protectionism and interference in the exchange-rate mechanism to achieve *autarchia*. But, in contrast to the Third Reich, the regime took some institutional steps towards developing a corporatist alternative to capitalism, more along the lines proposed by the Nationalists than the National Syndicalists, though it remained at an embryonic stage. In the event, Fascism's economic weaknesses, and hence military vulnerability, were decisive in preventing it from being a reliable Nazi ally and pulling its weight in the Axis.

Organic theories of corporate states, Catholic, authoritarian and fascist, were a feature of interwar Europe (Costa Pinto 2017), but the model advocated by Alexander Raven Thomson's *The Coming Corporate State* (1935) and adopted as official BUF policy would have produced a different economy again from the hybrid that emerged under Italian Fascism (Cerasi 2017). Some Iron Guard ideologues also adhered to corporatism in principle but (unlike their Fascist counterparts) saw it as a viable strategy to be adopted only *after* enacting the national revolution that would cleanse the nation of unwanted elements, mostly Jews (Moţa 1933: 3; Platon 2012). Nazism, on the other hand, improvised a changing blend of market economy and state planning on an ad hoc basis not anticipated in any of the corporatist models (Neumann 2017; Tooze 2006; Kershaw [1985] 2000: 47–69).

What sets Nazism apart from all other fascisms economically and morally, however, is that its racist permutation of fascism licensed it to create a vast European empire dependent to an increasing degree not just on the agricultural and economic production of conquered territories but, by the end of the war, on at least 12 million 'forced workers' or slaves subjected to various levels of dehumanization, exploitation, and both physical and mental torment. Some of these ended their days working for capitalist companies in factories built within concentration camps, such as the famous Buna works in Auschwitz, but the empathetic paradigm suggests it was dreams of Germany as a reborn ultra-nation, not capitalist schemes of increased profits, that had enslaved them.

The variety of fascist failure

A fundamental pattern in comparative studies in the 'fascist epoch' should now be emerging. Whatever topic is examined, it produces the picture of an extreme heterogeneity of phenomena at a surface or lived level coexisting with a fundamental homogeneity which comes into focus when attention shifts to the generic working definition or ideological matrix that is (metaphorically) generating the unique phenomenological realities. An optical image for this paradox would be a 3D lenticular poster showing two images: a memorable visual moment from the history of one particular fascist movement is seen from one viewing angle and the cover of a book on generic fascism from the other (e.g. this one!), allowing the viewer to flip between the two simply by shifting point of view.

The matrix was identified in the last chapter on the basis of methodological empathy as the pursuit of a new ultra-nation rising phoenix-like from a liberal society in crisis. The paradox of being able to see a unique political or historical phenomenon, such as the Holocaust, simultaneously as the manifestation of a generic concept (in this case 'genocide') resolves a protracted debate about whether Nazism was 'too unique' or 'extreme' to be treated as a form of fascism (Kershaw [1985] 2000: 20–46): it was *both* unique and *part* of an (ideal-typically constructed) genus of phenomena called 'fascism'. In fact, any topic within fascist studies, if examined comparatively, would manifest the same syndrome of extreme heterogeneity/particularity *and* homogeneity/'genericness', whether it concerned fascism's relationship to capitalism, anti-Semitism, established religion, political religion and ritual politics, demographic policies, popular traditions and customs, technocracy, work, the welfare state, painting, aesthetics, cinema, sport, architecture, education, mass organizations, masculinity, propaganda, social control, the law and the legal system, time, language, or any number of other specific issues. Roger Eatwell thus made an important theoretical contribution to understanding how diversity and homogeneity can be reconciled in comparative fascist studies when he argued that the same matrix of core ideals and goals could be expressed in the different clusters of beliefs and policies of individual movements operating within different historical habitats (Eatwell 1992, 2009).

Even within the same movement, radically contrasting positions were adopted on different policies within rival factions (Roberts 2000), and an examination of the worldviews of the Nazi leadership reveals deep divisions on key subjects such as anti-Semitism and the role of the peasantry in the new order (Kroll 1999). Yet, however bitter the disputes, all ideological or policy differences were generally accommodated within what was experienced *phenomeno-logically* as the 'same' movement (Platt 1980), founded on, and given cohesion by, the overarching myth of collective progress towards the people's imminent rebirth in the form of a modern ultra-nation ruled by a providential leader.

Concentrating on individual topics too closely, however, runs the risk of losing sight of yet another of fascism's outstanding generic traits as a new ideological force between 1918 and 1945, one which again assumes highly different forms but, in this case, becomes apparent only when the 'fascist epoch' is considered as a whole: its repeated failure as a revolutionary form of politics. Of the many fascist movements that surfaced in interwar Europe, only a handful can be said to have reached what Robert Paxton calls 'the rooting stage', where it is integrated into the country's political system, and only two, Fascism and Nazism, the (curiously phrased) 'arrival to/in power' stage, where they achieved a sustained degree of autonomous hegemony over the state and society in peacetime (Paxton 2004: chs 4, 5). The Croatian Ustasha, despite its genocidal violence, took power under the cover of war, remained ultimately dependent on the Axis powers, and quickly disintegrated with their defeat.

As for abortive movements, one, the Romanian Iron Guard, technically shared power – twice, in fact – before being repressed and finally eliminated, while others were reduced to the role of contributing to a puppet adminis-tration under Nazi occupation in France, Belgium, Holland, Denmark, Norway, Hungary and 'republican' Italy. Under authoritarian regimes, the rest were either crushed (e.g. in Salazar's Portugal), banned (in Vargas' Brazil) or absorbed (in Franco's Spain). Under liberal democracies, fascisms were marginalized everywhere except Italy and Germany (Griffin 1991: ch. 5). As for the eventual defeat of the founding Axis powers, Fascism, according to Paxton (2007: ch. 6) entered a phase of entropy in which it started to morph into a traditional authoritarian state, while Nazism's deepening radicalism led it to overreach itself in its military and imperi-alist ambitions and bring disaster on itself.

Historians have examined in detail the contingent factors that dictated that both Fascist Italy (Deakin 1962; De Grand

1991) and Nazi Germany (Kershaw 1999: chs 9–16; Evans 2004: chs 5–7) lost their way and were eventually defeated militarily. The crucial question in the present context is whether each failure of fascism, whether as an abortive movement or as a regime, was itself contingent and so counterfactually could have been avoided. Or was it instead the individual permutation of another basic aspect of the fascist matrix that generally prevents it from conquering the state in the first place, and, if it ever seizes power, *inevitably* condemns its attempts to realize its own ultranationalist utopias to give rise to dystopia and catastrophe, even if the precise *way* a fascist regime will fail remains contingent?

Once again, this book can only touch the surface of such a complex question, but a number of factors can be singled out which suggest that, irrespective of the profound contingency involved in *how* the regimes failed, the fascist project is always doomed to come to naught. The first obvious factor to be considered is the need for political space (Linz 1980) in order for a fascist groupuscule, or perhaps initially the revolutionary fantasy of a single individual, to make the transition to a movement with substantial populist momentum. Since authoritarian regimes have the power to close down threats to their hegemony by force, only liberal democratic regimes experiencing a profound crisis of legitimacy, one which has arisen in a nation undergoing an existential threat to its survival as an entire system, can allow a fascist movement to 'seize power' democratically. In the broadest sense, and in very different ways, this is the situation that Mussolini and Hitler were able to exploit, though both had previously used the threat of a paramilitary putsch with very different outcomes. A chronic lack of political space seals the fate of most fascist movements in their infancy – before and after 1945 – ensuring that the grapes of fascist wrath quickly wither on the vine. In fact, a major factor in the marginalization of fascism is the absence of a sufficiently profound and widespread *subjective* crisis of identification with the status quo within the mass of the population, however rife the *objective* factors of crisis may be (for a case study, see Cronin 1996).

As for the two regimes that did 'arrive in power', several generic factors doomed the Fascist and Nazi palingenetic ultra-nation to remain an extraordinarily costly fantasy for

humanity. First, in contrast to authoritarian and conservative regimes, fascist regimes depend for their viability on
a constant dynamism and extension of domestic and international power that no state can sustain. Second, territorial
ambitions will always lead to conflict, war and colonial
occupations, which, if no substantial economic benefit results
for the colonizer, cannot be maintained indefinitely without
bankrupting the country (as was going to be the case with
Fascist imperialism had defeat not intervened). Even if a
fascist empire is able to create a totalitarian empire and
run it using the resources seized and extracted by force
from its conquered enemies, as was the intention under the
Third Reich, it is subject to the law of 'the rise and fall of
Great Powers' identified by Paul Kennedy (1987), which
dictates they will always fail eventually for a combination
of economic, social, logistical and military reasons which
make them unsustainable. Furthermore, Nazism's obsession
with racial determinism meant its leaders were unlikely to
show the pragmatism that allowed the Roman and several
European colonial empires to be sustained for as long as they
were by creating citizens out of subjects.

Long before the inexorable decay of the Third Reich, its
power base and inner cohesion would have succumbed to the
major flaw of interwar fascism as a system of state power,
its dependency on a charismatic leader who is *by definition*
irreplaceable by any mechanism of succession unless a family
dynasty has been formed, a blind spot studiously ignored by
Mussolini and Hitler. But deeper factors condemned even the
most powerful fascist regime in history to last for little more
than twelve years of its proclaimed millennium of power: both
totalitarian regimes and their attempted totalist revolutions
were based on the possibility of socially engineering utopia,
and thus came aground and broke apart on the rocks of human
nature. Human beings are endowed with a protean self (Lifton
1993) which can neither be forcefully converted indefinitely to
an ideology nor permanently reduced to a compliant unit in
the scheme of hubris-ridden fantasists, no matter how much
suffering is inflicted and cruelty is applied by their henchmen.
The terror state is thus always a travesty of the revolutionary
and totalitarian utopia proclaimed in its own propaganda, and
the very attempt to realize its utopia through force and violence

is a grotesque failure of leadership and political intelligence. The anthropological and temporal revolutions spawned by fascist palingenetic fantasy will always be stillborn.

What this chapter has hopefully shown is that, to make the vast segment of modern history subsumed under the concept 'fascism' accessible to study and to interpretation as more than 'one damn thing after another' – or, as millions of non-fascists and victims actually experienced it, one horrific thing after another – it is vital for researchers to have recourse to a coherent generic concept, one which can serve as what has been called an 'interpretive grid', distinguishing fascism from non-fascisms and identifying repeated syndromes in ideas, policy and actions. Without one there is nothing to help researchers to decide what movements and regimes are to be classified as fascist or to make sense of material relating to events in so many disparate national histories. Equipped with such a grid, narrative patterns, common causal factors and interpretive pictures start to form spontaneously from the apparent randomness and contingency of facts. Such pictures resemble the shapes that mysteriously leap out from a 3D stereogram when the apparently meaningless abstract swirl of details and colours is not stared at, but stared *through*, so as to focus on a point *behind* the image (Levine and Priester 2008). The conceptual matrix we have proposed in the last chapter allows a profound homogeneity – invisible to those who insist that fascist scholars must simply stick to the facts and stop setting out on wild definitional goose chases – to emerge no less mysteriously from the welter of raw, and apparently random, data associated with fascism.

In the next chapter attention will shift to discerning how the same matrix of political utopianism that motivated so many uniformed fascist movements before 1945 was perpetuated in a profusion of highly diverse far-right phenomena which outwardly seem to have very little to do with interwar fascism. Though no longer able to mobilize crowds of hundreds of thousands, this variegated 'neo-fascism' has more than curiosity value to political scientists, since it still breeds hatred and is capable of inspiring targeted acts of discrimination and violence which make little sense outside the context of the original fascist visions of a new order born of the chaos of interwar Europe.

5
Neo-Fascism: Evolution, Adaption, Mutation

The threat to fascism posed by the Axis loss of the war

To move the focus of comparative fascist studies from interwar to postwar Europe is to enter an utterly transformed historical landscape. Between 1945 and 1955, the international political, social, economic and cultural order underwent structural changes no less profound, rapid and unexpected than those that combined in the wake of the First World War to create the original conditions for fascism to burst unannounced and unscripted onto the stage. But whereas fascism became, or at least behaved as, a contender for state power in several countries as the world crisis deepened in the 1930s, the consequences of the new wave of seismic upheavals which spread around the globe soon after the war proved lethal for fascism as a credible alternative to parliamentary democracy, conservative authoritarianism and communism.

In all but the former Axis powers, the rapid recovery of both liberalism and capitalism in Western and Northern Europe, at the same time as the emergence of the US and the USSR as rival superpowers locked in a potentially cataclysmic Cold War, severely restricted political space for revolutionary forms of nationalism as populist movements, whose rhetoric of national and racial renewal and rebirth

were in any case now utterly discredited. Using a phrase from
T. E. Lawrence's *The Seven Pillars of Wisdom*, Kevin Coogan
(1999) called Francis Yockey, an indefatigable campaigner
and undercover agent for an international fascist empire
to rise from the ashes of the war, a dangerous 'dreamer of
the day' (Yockey 1948). Since 1945, countless thousands of
obscure 'dreamers of the day', dispersed all over the world,
have spent their lives, alone or in small groups, vainly trying
to enact their updated version of a fascist utopia and refine
their own strategy for being a fascist in a post-fascist age, just
like more eminent unrepentant 'survivors' of the fascist era
such as Oswald Mosley (1968; Macklin 2007), Julius Evola
(1953, 1961; Furlong 2011: ch. 6), Maurice Bardèche (1961)
or Léon Degrelle (1969). Such loyalty to the cause has had to
be sustained in the face of the total military defeat of the Axis
powers in the European and Pacific theatres, at an overall
cost of over 70 million lives, and the revelation of millions of
horrendous crimes against civilians as a result of repression,
persecution and genocide committed in the name of a New
European Order or the Greater East Asia Co-Prosperity
Sphere – though imperial Japan was not technically fascist,
there were enough affinities for it to join the Axis powers
in 1937.

Ever since the Cold War began in the late 1940s, the winds
of historical change have been blowing fiercely against the
far right, making it all the more difficult to keep the flame
of their continued faith in ultranationalist rebirth burning
(the flame is a favourite fascist symbol). However confident
each fascist may remain in eventual 'victory', revolutionary
nationalism has been caught since the death of Mussolini
and Hitler in a perpetual political limbo, or what Armin
Mohler, one of the most influential neo-fascist intellectuals,
called, in his influential work *Die Konservative Revolution in
Deutschland 1918–1932* (1950), 'the interregnum': even for
believers, the awaited palingenesis has had to be postponed
indefinitely (Griffin 2000a, 2000b). Finding themselves
suddenly stranded in a hostile habitat, fascists were forced to
develop new species of organization now that the age of mass
'shirted' movements was over for the revolutionary right.

Even if Western liberal democracy had not recovered so
quickly against all the odds after the Axis defeat (Kershaw

2015), a drastic makeover of fascism (registered by the prefix 'neo-') was in any case inevitable once the vision of a new type of fascist ultra-state had become toxic and the language of race, eugenics and anti-Semitism that was identified with it in its Nazi variant had such repellent associations for the vast majority. This was especially true for the many millions of soldiers who had undergone the horrors not just of fighting against the Axis powers, but *for* them, and the many more civilians (including many millions of German nationals) who suffered directly or indirectly the consequences of both the Axis and the Allied military campaigns. Gruesome images from the liberation of Belsen-Bergen concentration camp and the ovens of Auschwitz were branded into the collective historical memory for generations to come, making anti-fascism a default position in the West for liberal democrats and the left. The attempt by Western idealists to reinstate the hegemony of humanism was symbolized in the publication by the newly founded UNESCO in 1950 of the first of four statements on 'the race question'. Its preamble affirmed: 'The great and terrible war that has now ended was a war made possible by the denial of the democratic principles of the dignity, equality and mutual respect of men, and by the propagation, in their place, through ignorance and prejudice, of the doctrine of the *inequality* of men and races' (UNESCO 1969). The fascist epoch was over for good, and the omens for neo-fascism were bleak.

The contentiousness of 'neo-fascism'

However, as with every other aspect of fascism, the issue, and the very existence, of a 'neo-fascism' as it is being presented here is debatable. It is thus particularly important for readers unfamiliar with the topic, and venturing into this particularly complex area of political phenomena for essay purposes, to understand how the account of it given in this chapter fits into the book's overall thesis and 'narrative'.

From what has already been said, the most obvious objection to be addressed is that, by talking about fascism in evolutionary terms as a genus 'adapting' and 'evolving' after 1945 and entering a new phase of speciation, its status is being significantly altered here by verbal sleight of hand. Instead, of being simply a conceptual construct derived from a process of ideal-typical abstraction, sceptics might claim it is now being reified, and, worse still, *biologized*, and thus turned into a life form capable of cycles of sickness and health, of survival and extinction and of evolutionary mutation, in a discourse curiously reminiscent of how the fascists organicized the nation. But such charges are easily dismissed. It has already been pointed out that language possesses an in-built tendency to reify and anthropomorphize once a generic concept is used in academic discourse. A history of capitalism, socialism, feudalism, warfare, dictatorship or terrorism cannot help but produce sentences which suggest they are entities behaving biologically: 'growing', 'falling', 'spreading', 'receding', and so on. Fortunately, the analytical context makes it clear that such 'personification' is nothing more sinister than a conceptual shorthand. Thus when, in his preface to *The Coming of the Third Reich*, Richard Evans talks of the 'rise' and 'triumph' of Nazism and Stalinism (2004: xxvii), it would be absurd to accuse him of treating Nazism as an organism endowed with its own supra-individual life-force (a fascist way of thinking).

Readers are thus asked to remember what was said in chapter 3 in the discussion of ideal types – that 'generic fascism is a construct, an empty conceptual shell, and has no independent or organic life of its own.' In other words, the personified or organic metaphors used about postwar fascism in this chapter are simply that: metaphors. They communicate the narrative of fascism's evolution which emerges when approached on the basis of the empathetic paradigm. They should not be turned by the mind's propensity for dramatization into an animate, supra-individual 'force', like the swirling green and purple mists of envy and evil which whipped up Moscow's underclass into rebellion against the Romanovs in Walt Disney's *Anastasia* (1997).

A more substantial objection could be made about whether the topic of 'neo-fascism' merits a chapter to itself, on a par with interwar fascism. After all, a number of books purporting to be about generic fascism ignore the topic of postwar developments altogether (e.g. De Felice 1977;

Carsten 1967) or treat neo-fascism as a sort of epilogue to the main story, which can produce some interesting general reflections on fascism's failure to thrive after 1965 (e.g. Payne 1995: 496–522; Mann 2004: 265–75; Paxton 2004: 172–205). At the other end of the scale, militant Marxists typically see fascism at work in any form of organized racism, xenophobia, Islamophobia or discrimination, such as anti-immigrant protests, G8 conferences and all forms of anti-left authoritarianism, attributing it to capitalism's latent tendency to breed social exclusion and discrimination. The way journalists and politicians bandy the term 'fascism' around does not help create a sober atmosphere of forensic inquiry either. No wonder some non-Marxists, notably James Gregor (2006), have voiced their scepticism about the whole notion of 'neo-fascism' and criticized the 'abuse of social science' in its pursuit. Even well-disposed 'liberal' political scientists might disagree with the taxonomy offered here and wish to include 'right-wing populism' and jihadism within its scope. However, they would perhaps exclude the European New Right and Russian Eurasianism, because they do not overtly advocate violence, or disqualify white noise music and punk racism as theatrical rather than political in inspiration, even though, as will be argued later, there are grounds for taking both seriously as rejections of liberal democratic values and expressions of political utopianism shaped by palingenetic ultranationalist fantasy.

In the present context 'fascism' must be carefully disentangled from 'populism', since its allegedly growing threat to democracy is often mistaken for a sign of the spread of fascism, and, moreover, my own definition talks of 'populist ultranationalism'. It is thus worth stressing that, in academic analysis and properly researched journalism, 'populism', or more precisely 'the populist radical right', is generally used to designate an illiberal but democratic and *non-revolutionary* form of politics driven by widespread (hence 'popular') mistrust of ruling political and economic elites, both domestic and international. This mistrust is compounded by concerns about the impact on national identity and sovereignty of globalizing forces such as multiculturalism, international trade, the export of manufacturing jobs, and mass immigration (Moffitt 2016).

A penetrating analysis by David Goodhart (2017) suggests that the driving force behind populism is not the fascist longing for an ultra-nation, but anomie, the feeling of vague existential threat stemming from modernity itself, of being a stranger in your own country, the longing to have roots, to have an identity, and to be 'somewhere' familiar, not to live in the new world of the revolutionary imaginary. Such 'Somewheres' want to ensure the nation's democracy and the human rights it guarantees are enjoyed only by the 'home' ethnicity (producing a form of 'ethnocratic liberalism') and that the national culture is not contaminated by 'foreign' influences. They thus inhabit a different phenomenological universe to 'Anywheres', who feel at ease in a rootless, centreless postmodern world of multiculturalism, foreign travel for business, and the liminal spaces of airports, exotic restaurants and conference hotels depicted in the film *Up in the Air* (2009). Anywheres may be a demographic minority but constitute a majority within political, educational, professional and economic elites. Following this line of argument, populism is to be distinguished both ideologically and psychologically from fascism, which is not to say that some right-wing populist parties in Europe do not attract votes from 'genuine' fascists. To use the legal distinction applied by the German constitutional law, right-wing populism is 'radical', and hence legal, in contrast to fascism, which is 'extreme', and hence illegal.

As for the notion that neo-fascism is a mere footnote to interwar fascism, certainly if it is defined primarily in terms of a charismatic leader, a militia-party, shirted paramilitaries, ritual politics, territorial expansionism and virulent anti-communism, then it indeed hardly merits attention. But the position adopted in this book is first that, having offered a definition which makes sense of fascism in its 'epoch' in terms of its myth of ultranationalist rebirth, it is important for several reasons to offer some idea of how to follow through the story of revolutionary nationalism into the postwar era. First, there is the legitimate human curiosity to see what became of such a potent force for destruction and calculated inhumanity, especially in its Nazi and Croatian manifestations, after 1945. Second, there is surely some degree of professional responsibility on the part of experts on fascism to establish *forensically* its structural links with other recent forms of right-wing extremism, notably the extremist ethnic separatism of the sort manifested in the Balkan Wars, in various ethnically, culturally or religiously inspired terrorist acts, campaigns and wars – including those committed by 'lone wolves' such as Timothy McVeigh and Anders Breivik. Third, it is important in the context of the European Union's bid to create a harmonious multicultural international society that experts understand and evaluate the threat posed to democracy by contemporary extreme right-wing movements such as Hungary's Jobbik, Greece's Golden Dawn and Slovakia's People's Party Our Slovakia (LSNS), all of which, as we shall see, display strong neo-fascist elements. It might also be useful if experts on fascism were called upon for their insights at least by the media and civil servants to deconstruct historically vacuous accusations of 'fascism' that some diplomats level at each other during territorial disputes.

Fourth, only on the basis of deep historical knowledge and careful scholarly analysis (which needs to be collaborative) is it possible to monitor fascism's development in its various forms, reconstruct their genealogy and networks, and offer informed – *empirically grounded and conceptually coherent* – assessments of the prospects that something resembling interwar fascism (though in a different guise) may return as a virulent force in individual countries, or even as an international scourge. Unfortunately, these are not qualities to be found in most newspaper articles, blogs, documentaries, books or pronouncements by politicians that have been published in the last five decades warning of fascism's imminent resurgence (e.g. Eisenberg 1967; Goslan 1998; Lee 1999).

Finally, understanding neo-fascism is also important for illuminating any structural links that might exist between it and political Islam's 'war on the West' and jihadism in general – sometimes misleadingly called 'Islamofascism'. The key point to emerge from our analysis is that, even at its most ritualistic and cultic, fascism cannot go beyond sacralizing extreme nationalist and racist politics, both of which have their roots in the rapidly secularizing society of nineteenth-century Europe. It remains a secular force and thus remains distinct from Islamist terrorism, which represents an extreme form of the *politicization and secularization of a religion* which can be traced back to the origins of Islam itself. The fact that some neo-Nazis, notably Ahmed Huber and David Myatt, have been so impressed by the success of Islamist attacks on the West since 9/11 that they have converted to Islam and adopted Muslim names (Michael 2006) does not imply a basic affinity between the two creeds.

The failure of neo-fascism as a populist revolutionary force

The strength the populist right in the US and Europe since the 1980s at a time when revolutionary ultranationalism remains so stubbornly marginalized as a contender for state power highlights a central paradox in the recent history of fascism. It has failed to gain significant popular traction in Europe and the US, which condemns it to remain at a stunted, 'pre-movement' stage of development in all its manifestations as far as its bid to have a transformative impact on history is concerned. This revolutionary impotence has prevailed since 1945, despite a superabundance of conditions and factors which could theoretically have led to a pervasive sense of decline and existential threat to collective identities, whether national, civilizational or racial, and hence the belief that establishing a healthy ultra-nation is the only way to solve them. They include the global economic crisis of 2007–8 and its long-term effects, especially the high levels of unemployment in most Western countries for many of the young, who have little prospect of work or material security – and this at a time when the spread of consumerism, the globalization of an Americanized culture, and the 'religion' of materialism still gains ground and secularization continues apace. There is also a widespread crisis of personal identity and purpose driving an epidemic of addiction of many forms, one symptom of which is the entrenchment of an increasingly lethal drug and alcohol culture among the world's youth – all lived out against the background of major structural challenges to traditional national and cultural homogeneity.

Prominent among these is the visibly growing strength of Islam in many (formerly) Christian Europeanized countries, while shattering socio-economic and humanitarian crises in many Asian, Middle Eastern, Central African and Latin American countries, often exacerbated by the impact of war, are leading to many millions attempting to reach Europe and the US as economic migrants or political refugees. The chronic decline of the industrial and manufacturing base in Europe and the US against the background of the rise of China as an economic superpower, the prospect of a second Cold War with Russia, the free movement of millions from (at present) twenty-seven nationalities to wherever they have work within the European Union, the growing evidence of ecological and demographic crisis, the yawning gap between capitalist and ruling elites and ordinary people ... readers can add to the list themselves. Even what for liberals are positive developments, such as the emancipation of the LGBT community, the rise of multicultural tolerance, and the work undertaken by NGOs to create a more just global society, are considered by some on the far right as symptoms of moral decadence.

Yet despite this plethora of what interwar fascists would have interpreted as evidence of a civilization in crisis, neo-fascism, with the exception of the three fascist party-political movements established in Hungary, Greece and Slovakia, remains overwhelmingly confined to a marginalized subculture in every society, reduced to holding rallies and carrying out constant propaganda campaigns and sporadic physical attacks on 'demonized others' – which is not to minimize the devastating, and sometimes lethal, impact of such aggression on individuals and targeted communities. Overt displays of revolutionary nationalist passions are so taboo in the West that Islamophobic or anti-Islamization movements, such as the English Defence League (EDL), Stop Islamization of Europe (SIOE) or Pegida (from the German acronym for 'Patriotic Europeans against the Islamization of the West'), go to some lengths to dissociate themselves from neo-Nazism. The effect of this is that these movements act in practice as the activist factions of radical right-wing populist parties such as the French National Front and Alternative for Germany and are not symptoms of 'the rise of fascism' (though the radical left would disagree with this categorization).

This is not to deny that a small but vociferous hard-core of potentially violent neo-fascists is actively involved in various parts of the world in a struggle against the 'genocide' of their nation through mass migration, multiculturalism and Islamization, and loss of national sovereignty to supranational bodies such as the European Union and the United Nations all over the Westernized world. But the organization of the first 'hate rock fest' by Tom Metzger in 1988, attended by a few hundred white supremacists, or even the 'Right Rock' festival held in Thüringen in 2017, which attracted some 6,000 hard-core neo-Nazis keen to share their anger at the ethnic plight of Germany, should be seen in a broader perspective. Even if the partially white supremacist 'alt-right' made a media splash with their support for Trump in 2016, and there were some 12,000 violence-prone right-wing extremists known to German authorities in 2017, such figures should be placed against the fact that over 50,000 Ku Klux Klan members marched on Washington in 1925 (Roberts 2012), and that in January 1932 the SA, the Nazi paramilitary force, numbered 400,000. Even more telling, in Germany over 100,000 have turned out to protest *against* a Pegida demonstration of 20,000 (Huggler 2015).

The films of silent torch-lit processions through German towns of the 'Immortals' movement, its marchers wearing identical, expressionless theatrical masks, went viral on social media in 2012 and deliberately evoked a scene in the documentary *The Triumph of the Will*. The visual suggestion that Nazism was a dormant force about to awaken to save Germany from the threats to its culture was a powerful publicity image, but it was advertising a dead cause: the federal state simply banned the movement. The contrast with the Weimar Republic could not be more graphic. The instant rise and equally instant fall of *Die Unsterblichen* is emblematic of the acute marginalization and structural weakness of neo-fascism as a force in contemporary world politics compared with the interwar period. The systematic failure of 'movement', let alone party-political, neo-fascism can be largely attributed to the striking absence, at least when compared to Weimar in 1929–33, of a generalized subjective sense of an existential crisis of the nation and of modern liberal civilization profound enough to create ample political space for radical alternatives based on myths of national, racial and cultural homogeneity and renewal. What little space might have been available has been taken up either by radical and extreme right-wing populism or by the encroachment on public space by private and virtual space that effectively depoliticizes modern life.

A sustained internet search into neo-fascism might seem to contradict this insistence on its impotence, even when populism and Islamism are removed from the equation. The impression could quickly be formed that neo-fascism has in fact shown extraordinary resilience to have survived the defeat of the Axis by over seventy years – six times as long as the Third Reich – leading to the proliferation of parties, movements and groups all over the world, and generating many thousands of searchable headings and names on the World Wide Web referring to individuals and groups which together constitute a permanent subculture of right-wing extremism largely resistant to prosecution. Yet the apparent abundance of neo-fascist phenomena is actually the sign of advanced fragmentation and impotence compared with the 'era of fascism', when an alliance of just two of its variants, Fascism and Nazism, profoundly threatened the hegemony of liberal democracy and Soviet communism and plunged the world into war for five years.

The sheer number of minuscule neo-fascist parties and organizations with a presence in cyberspace is more reminiscent of the splintering of the minute and hopelessly ineffectual Judean resistance to Roman occupation portrayed in Monty Python's *The Life of Brian* (1979). The vast majority of groups pursuing palingenetic fantasies of national or racial regeneration that have come into existence in many parts of the world since 1945, often far outside fascism's original heartlands, have achieved only insignificant and ephemeral active membership, received negligible public support, and disappeared without trace (though not neces- sarily without causing genuine intimidation and hate crimes in local areas in the brief span of their existence). A group that sounds so powerful and ambitious on its website will usually turn out to be maintained by a handful of enthusiasts with a defective reality principle, trapped in self-delusion and bereft of practical influence, no matter how many visits, posted comments or 'likes' the site can boast in the age of cyberfascism.

Symptomatic of neo-fascism's systemic failure as a politically effective mass movement were Britain First's leaders' abortive attempts in the mid-2010s to turn its 500,000 Facebook likes into a mass movement to 'take [their] country back'. The rallies they held could attract only a couple of hundred flesh and blood supporters, who were vastly outnumbered by protesters and police. Without the critical mass of embodied and activist support necessary to project mass palingenetic expectancy onto a secular saviour figure, who then directs and coordinates their assault on 'the system', there can be no genuine charismatic leader of fascism in the postwar period. This reduces the would-be *Führer* to a fantasist, a leader without followers, in charge of a movement that does not move – a situation explored in Daniel Ragussi's film *Imperium* (2016), which illustrates the utter isolation and desperate fantasy politics of postwar neo-Nazi groupuscules, organizations with a web presence that may suggest a powerful force for change but actually have a handful of members and are often run on a shoe-string.

Another symptom of neo-fascism's structural failure is the separation out into disparate elements of a number of components that had been able to coalesce organically within the Nazi movement because of the sheer size and populist energy of its numerical support after 1929. The leadership, the electoral party, its paramilitary wing, the party ideologues, its propaganda machine, its cultural visionaries and intellectuals, its thugs, its henchmen and hit-men have disaggregated in the hostile climate since 1945 and taken on an independent life of their own. To offer an overview of neo-fascism thus requires breaking the topic down into individual components familiar from its interwar species only as integral parts of movements. After this, attention will turn to several permutations of neo-fascism unimaginable in the interwar period and instrumental to its survival now.

The failure of the postwar fascist party

After the war, there were attempts in both European countries that had formed the Axis to create national 'parties' that would perpetuate the national fascist cause from within the newly re-established democratic systems. The Movimento Sociale Italiano (MSI) brought together from the north former intransigent *Repubblichini* from the anti-clerical and anti-monarchist Italian Social Republic (RSI) (Quartermaine 2000) with unreconstructed Fascists from the south, still nostalgic for the first incarnation of Mussolini's *ventennio*, or two Fascist decades. Once it had shed its revolutionary baggage and the rhetoric of Italy's imminent rebirth, the MSI entered the parliamentary system as an outwardly respectable centre-right party and was soon fully integrated within the Italian party system alongside the Christian Democrats (DC) and the (no less de-revolutionized) Italian Communist Party (PCI). The three continued to wheel and deal in their domination of national political life until the 'Clean Hands' anti-corruption campaign forced them all into dissolution in the 1990s.

In the meantime, the MSI adapted to the new hegemony of Western democracy by developing a refined double-speak (Feldman and Jackson 2014), a coded discourse in which policies and manifesto promises were crafted to allow the initiated still to discern echoes of interwar dreams of epic grandeur, while the uninitiated could choose to take the exoteric rhetoric at their democratic face value. For example, the MSI's eventual support for NATO and the EU was received esoterically by nostalgic Fascists not as a pragmatic capitulation to the new world order, but in terms of support for a 'European nationalism' whose roots lay in pan-fascist support for the Axis fight to defend the continent against American and Russian occupation (Griffin 2008). MSI propaganda posters reveal a continued commitment to a future modelled on the Fascist glory days, a message summed up in the slogan of its leader in the 1970s, Giorgio Almirante, the RSI's former head of propaganda: 'Nostalgia for the Future' (Cheles 1991).

Party-based neo-Nazism fared no better in Germany. The Soviet-controlled German Democratic Republic (GDR) was largely purged of Nazi activism from the outset, while fascism was presented as a cancerous growth endemic to capitalism, in line with Comintern orthodoxy. In the newly constituted German Federal Republic, the horrors of the war and the spontaneous embrace of the values of civil society during the reconstruction years of the 'miracle economy' ensured that only a small minority locked in denial about the realities of the Third Reich actively worked to resuscitate the pre-war Nazi movement. However, once the war generation passed, neo-Nazism was to become established as a major outlet for adolescent discontent and angst, disaffected youths embracing its racial creed and insignia to express their rejection of multiculturalism, mass immigration and 'the system', rather than in a serious display of revolutionary commitment to a new nationalist order (which is why some experts believe neo-Nazism should not be treated seriously as a form of neo-fascism). The thinly veiled attempt to relaunch the NSDAP, first as the German Reich Party (1950) and then, in 1964, as the National Democratic Party (NPD), was thus doomed from the start, and both were condemned to hover on the fringe of legality without ever crossing Germany's 5 per cent minimum threshold for representation in the federal parliament (Nagle 1970). Though the NPD managed a small rise in support after the vast influx of refugees into Germany in 2015–16, its neo-fascism was overshadowed by the populism of the non-revolutionary Alternative for Germany.

Outside Italy and Germany, neo-fascist parties have remained even more irrelevant to the mainstream political life of most European democracies, unable to rehabilitate the rhetoric of extreme nationalism after the horrors of the Third Reich. To take Britain as an example, Mosley's Union Movement, formed in 1948, proved impotent to turn to its advantage the growing xenophobia roused by the postwar influx of Afro-Caribbean immigrants and the arrivals *en masse* of other ethnic minorities, and so suffered consistently disastrous defeats at the polls until its final dissolution in 1994. Meanwhile, even at the peak of its street and media presence in 1979, when it exploited both severe economic and political dislocation and rising anxiety about immigration, the National Front could win only 0.6 per cent of the vote in the national election that brought Margaret Thatcher to power. Her accession as a prime minister, perceived (erroneously) as signalling a new toughness on immigration, spelt the end of the minuscule resurgence of fascism in Britain as an electoral force. This, along with the rise of the United Kingdom Independence Party (UKIP) as a rival outlet for identitarian politics in the 2000s, ensured that Nick Griffin's attempted 'modernization' of the British National Party to disguise its neo-Nazi credentials and corner the right-wing populist vote made no headway (Copsey 1996; Griffin 1996). When, in 2015, voters in the UK general election were faced with a choice between a genuine right-wing populist party and a neo-Nazi imitation, it was the BNP that failed miserably at the polls, while UKIP triumphed (Copsey 2007; Mudde 2007; Mudde and Kaltwasser 2017).

A similar pattern can be seen in the fate of the MSI in Italy, at one time the largest neo-fascist party in the world. Once it was turned into the right-wing populist National Alliance, intransigent fascists decided to form the Fiamma Tricolore (the flame again!) to keep the true Fascist tradition alive – and promptly disappeared from the radar. This pattern of failure is repeated in most former communist states – for instance, in Romania, which had witnessed the rise of the Legion of the Archangel Michael (Iron Guard) into a major populist political force during the 1930s. The overthrow of Ceauşescu led to the appearance of several minuscule and ineffectual parties claiming the mantel of its genuinely charismatic leader, Corneliu Codreanu, such as the Iron Guard, All for the Fatherland (another name of the Iron Guard), For the Fatherland, and the New Right. As a party-political force, then, neo-fascism is largely irrelevant to postwar politics.

The exceptionalism of Ukraine, Hungary, Greece and Slovakia

If some pro-Russian commentators and politicians were to be believed, Ukraine is the main exception to this pattern. By the mid-2010s, they would argue, neo-fascism had actually succeeded in penetrating parliamentary life to a point where the whole government could be accused of Nazism. The allegations centre on the rise of Svoboda (Freedom), which held thirty-seven parliamentary seats between 2012 and 2014 and briefly secured three ministerial positions in 2014, including that of deputy prime minister. Certainly, both Svoboda and the small paramilitary party Right Sector had members at the time of the Ukraine–Russia crisis who looked back nostalgically to the militant patriotism that led a section of the population to collaborate temporarily in 1941–4 with the Wehrmacht, Schutzmannschaft, Reichskommissariat Ukraine and SS and to engage in brutal, proto-genocidal ethnic cleansing of Poles and Jews in the west of the country. Certainly, the territorial conflicts with Russia – which has an important neo-fascist and populist radical right subculture of its own (Umland 2015) – have exacerbated the rhetoric of militant patriotism and the rise of nationalist paramilitarism in the name of defending Ukraine from the serious threat posed there by the ongoing separatist movement of ethnic Russians unofficially backed by the Russian army.

Yet in practice, whatever their distant roots in Ukrainian fascism, both parties function as movements of the populist radical right, and sometimes just the populist right, rather than of revolutionary nationalism. A demonstration of this is Svoboda's active participation in the pro-European, pro-democratic protests in 2013, as well as its subsequent support for the ratification of the Association Agreement with the EU. It also backed constitutional reform to limit the president's powers, just at the time when their polls suggested Svoboda's leader, Oleh Tyahnybok, would win 28.8 per cent of the popular vote. In any case, by 2017 its electoral support had shrunk to under 5 per cent, which hardly makes Ukraine a Nazi country (Shekhovtsov 2016).

There are, however, three countries where fascist electoral parties have had more success in becoming an integral part of the 'political system' without totally sacrificing their extremist identity: Greece, Hungary and Slovakia. After it registered as a political party in 1993 with extravagant irredentist ambitions for Greece in the Balkans, which was at that time dissolving into warring ethnic and religious factions, the Golden Dawn acquired several components that for a time made it Europe's most high-profile emulation of an interwar fascist movement.

These included an elaborate myth of national rebirth based on the alleged qualities of Hellenic civilization but reformulated in terms of (Nazi) Aryan biological racism; a nostalgia for the para-fascist, ultranationalist dictatorial regime of Metaxas in the 1930s (Kallis 2010); and a political religion consisting of Roman salutes, intimidating torch-lit rallies, the celebration of symbolic days in the history of the nation, and the saturation of public spaces with flags bearing the ancient Greek symbol for eternity, deliberately designed to evoke the Nazi Swastika (Vasilopoulou and Halikiopoulou 2015). As for its ideology, it pours out its vitriol on all the usual suspects, appealing to populist xenophobia, anti-Americanism and, particularly since the Greek government debt crisis began in 2009, anti-EU and anti-German sentiment. This it combines with a visceral hatred of communism, international (Jewish) capitalism and consumerism, as well as the liberal (Jewish) intelligentsia and cultural cosmopolitanism.

But it is perhaps in its determination to function as a 'mass-militia party' that the Golden Dawn reveals its profound nostalgia for the era of fascism, wooing support in electoral campaigns at the same time as its activists were cultivating collaborative links with the security services and prepared to murder the left-wing rapper Pavlos Fyssas in an emulation of SA violence under the Nazis. After 2012, the combination of the deepening economic woes of Greece with the massive influx of refugees from Syria, Asia, Africa and beyond created a perfect storm for fuelling extremism. Yet despite the highly favourable conjuncture of factors, its leader Nikolaos Michaloliakos has never acquired more than 'coterie charisma', which exists only for the party faithful (Eatwell 2006), and in the EU elections of 2014 party support peaked at under 10 per cent. Significantly, the party actually lost support after the killing of Fyssas.

In contrast, the same elections saw Jobbik become Hungary's third largest party, with over 20 per cent of the vote, even though it was up against the dominant right-of-centre Fidesz party. Fidesz had itself moved significantly towards anti-EU, anti-multicultural, anti-immigration and anti-liberal policies (which by 2017 included the closing of borders and attacks on basic liberal freedoms), thereby reducing the political space available for right-wing extremism. By 2016 Jobbik's leader, Gábor Vona, the former head of the now banned paramilitary unit Magyar Gárda Mozgalom, had perfected the 'doublespeak' demanded of all neo-fascist parties since 1945 if they are to survive. While Vona has worked hard to play down the party's racist, anti-Semitic and extremist image in the media and to keep the party officially within the fold of the populist radical right, Jobbik militants have continued to perform elaborate political rituals evoking the interwar anti-liberal, anti-communist, anti-Semitic, anti-Roma era of the Horthy regime (and, by association, Ferenc Szálasi's Hungarist and collaborationist Arrow Cross). Meanwhile, many of its ideologues still disseminate overtly anti-Semitic and irredentist messages, and its party literature maintains the Turanian myth promulgated in the 1930s by Hungarism that the country's organic nationhood derived from its non-European origins as a Central Asian tribe – for Szálasi, even Christ was of Turanian extraction. Such ambivalence allows Jobbik to be voted for either as a populist radical right-wing party or as a neo-fascist party whose revolutionary vanguard, despite the ban, is still 'present' in spirit at its emotional and ideological core.

This ambiguity, no less vital to the continued success of France's Front National as a simultaneously hard (radical) right and moderate right party, is symptomatic of fascism's adaptation to what former MSI leader Gianfranco Fini, in his speech to the newly formed National Alliance in April 1994, referred to as a 'post-fascist' age. The extremist roots of Jobbik, and to a lesser extent of the Front National, have left the aura of fascism hovering around the two parties for those who want to see it, no matter how careful they are not to behave like an interwar fascist movement in public arenas (Blomqvist et al. 2013).

The most recent symptom of the potential vitality of party-political neo-fascism is the rise of the People's Party Our Slovakia (LSNS). This is attributable partly to the personal charisma (for his followers) of its leader, Marián Kotleba, who in 2013 became Europe's first openly neo-Nazi provincial governor. The LSNS won thirteen parliamentary seats in 2016 after a campaign characterized by crude hate-speech directed at ethnic minorities and allusions to the extermination campaigns of the Third Reich as a solution to the country's problems (Nociar 2017). All these parties, as well as any right-wing populist party with an extreme fringe, need to be closely monitored for links to right-wing violence and terrorism which should bar them from the democratic process if liberalism is to retain hegemony.

The cultic milieu of groupuscular neo-fascism

Apparently, there are over 20,000 pieces of satellite debris larger than an orange orbiting the Earth. A similar figure probably exists for the number of extreme right-wing groupuscules, larger and smaller, more or less ephemeral, more or less obscure, that have come into existence since 1945. In their various ways they cultivate fantasies of a revolutionary national or international order made up of healthy organic peoples, purged of decadence and brimming with renewed communal strength and state power drawn from their primordial cultural or racial taproots. These too can be thought of as debris, shards of what might have been much larger-scale utopian projects that fragmented catastrophically after the destruction of the Axis at the hands of the same Anglo-British and Soviet powers that they had consistently demonized and underestimated as their culturally and racially inferior enemies.

To survey them in a synoptic introduction to a key concept such as this and to single out particular ones for comment is problematic, because each country has its own dynamically shifting extreme right milieu shaped by unique historical conditions. For example, Alexander Ross (2017) offers a fascinating left-wing take on the vigorous, heterogeneous but still highly marginalized fascist subculture that has grown up in the US in the post-1945 era, its deep roots both in interwar European fascism and America's long homegrown tradition of white supremacy and colonialism and its extensive contemporary entanglements with the populist (and hence democratic) right mobilized by Donald Trump. Although reasons of space make a comprehensive account of the global forms of neo-fascist organization and activity that have emerged since 1945 impossible, a concise survey will allow us to highlight the sheer abundance of groupuscular activity, which is, as we have argued, a symptom both of neo-fascism's weakness and of its strength.

Taken individually, the support base of any one organization may seem so minuscule as to be irrelevant to a country's political life, even when it is a relatively mature and sophisticated one, such as the neo-fascist Paris-based Groupe Union Défense (GUD). Openly associating itself with the Celtic cross, the symbol of international white supremacy, GUD was first created as a response to the left-wing student protests in Paris during the 'Events' of May 1968. Five decades on, it now maintains a professional Web presence used for summoning the faithful to its meetings, coordinating 'actions', and providing a neo-fascist commentary on current affairs, but it hardly ever breaks into headline news.

However, once groupuscular formations such as GUD (Griffin 1999), Nouvelle Résistance (Bale 2002), National Socialist Underground (Koehler 2014), Casa-Pound (Castelli Gattinara and Froio 2014), the Nordic Resistance Movement in Norway, Sweden, Finland and Iceland, the UK's National Action (banned in 2016) and the far more tenacious White Aryan Resistance (WAR) in the US are seen as single pixels of a much bigger picture – small nodes in a far-flung network of highly disparate, loosely linked neo-fascist radicalism operating throughout the Westernized world – they reveal a deeper significance. The aggregate effect of many thousands of such groupuscules, however ephemeral individually, is to function as a dynamic, international 'cultic milieu', which allows those who join one to feel part of an esoteric 'order' and charged with a clandestine political task which can become like a sacred mission to them. The fascist terrorist Timothy McVeigh, for example, was influenced by the fictional white supremacist underground organization 'the Order', portrayed in *The Turner Diaries* (Pearce [1978] 2013), describing a racial Armageddon, which also inspired a violent neo-Nazi groupuscule of the same name. It is also no coincidence if occultism and pagan mysteries play a role in some neo-fascist groups (Goodrick-Clarke 2003; Kaplan 1997).

The cumulative effect of the international groupuscular right is to form a permanent latent 'oppositional subculture' (Kaplan and Lööw 2002) through which thousands may pass on their path to radicalization. Moreover, in an internet-savvy age, each groupuscule can ensure it is only the click of a mouse away from nudging someone already predisposed to extreme nationalism into further fanaticism and, in extreme cases, into crossing the Rubicon from compensatory fantasy to violent activism.

In contrast to interwar militia parties, much groupuscular fascism is a vanguard phenomenon which does not court populist support or cultivate charismatic leadership, following instead the principles of 'leaderless resistance' (Beam 1992; Griffin 2003b). As quickly as formations disappear in the micro-environment of the far right's cultic milieu, new ones can emerge, thus maintaining the network's intensity as a radicalizing influence while placing it largely beyond the monitoring powers, let alone the control, of the security services. To take two examples of its effectiveness as a transmitter of extremism in the UK context, it was the internet contact of the extreme loner David Copeland (also influenced by *The Turner Diaries*) with David Myatt's National Socialist Movement in the 1990s that helped convince him to launch what has misleadingly come to be known as a 'lone wolf' terrorist campaign (Gable and Jackson 2011) by using a series of nail-bombs in London to incite a race war (McLagen and Lowles 2000). Two decades later, it would be the regular exposure of Thomas Mair, living in a quiet Yorkshire town, to *National Vanguard*, the magazine of the US neo-fascist groupuscule National Alliance, that helped catalyse his eventual metamorphosis in 2016 from neo-Nazi fantasist to homicidal terrorist as the murderer of the MP Jo Cox. Supercharged by the power of the internet, the neo-fascist cultic milieu fosters apocalyptic fantasies of imminent or postponed ultranationalist rebirth brought about through violence against a decadent society, so providing an antidemocratic hinterland to the more outwardly democratic landscape of neo-fascist and radical right populist parties.

The postwar internationalization of fascism

The internet also gives added momentum to a trend within groupuscular neo-fascism which has become far more prevalent since the fascist era: internationalization. In the 1930s, individual ideologues such as Drieu la Rochelle (Soucy 1979), José Streel (1942) and Ezra Pound (Feldman 2013) were already presenting fascism as a pan-European force of rebirth, and doomed attempts were made by some of Mussolini's followers, convinced of their movement's 'universal' civilizational significance, to create a Fascist International (Ledeen 1972; Kallis 2016).

With the war apparently going Hitler's way, an entire bureaucracy was set up by the Third Reich to plan the postwar European New Order (Herzstein 1982), and, in more desperate circumstances, a major theme of Nazi and Fascist propaganda in the last two years of the war was the struggle to save Europe from destruction by the US and the USSR. Recent scholarship in comparative fascist studies has also begun to uncover another rich case study in the intensely transnational dimension of fascism by analysing the intimate contacts and entangled histories of Italian and Spanish revolutionary ultranationalists both before and after the war (Albanese and del Hierrero 2016). Though much still has to be done to be able to map accurately the diffusion of both Fascism and Nazism through the creation of the many interwar movements which, like Anton Mussert's National Socialist Movement (NSB) in Holland and Oswald Mosley's BUF, hybridized their influence with indigenous currents of ultranationalism, the idea of interwar fascism as an exclusively national phenomenon has long been superseded.

Little wonder, then, that after 1945 fascism was frequently presented by its most fervent idealists who had survived the war as a struggle not just for a national but for a *European* rebirth, a theme crystallized in Mosley's policy of 'Europe a nation', the formation of the New European Order and the foundation of the journal *Nation Europe*, all dating from 1951 (Griffin 2008). Meanwhile, the inveterate US Nazi sympathizer and anti-Semite Francis Yockey, referred to earlier, had taken up an intensely peripatetic life to realize his vision of a new fascist international order, this time including the US, which would refute Oswald Spengler's predictions of the West's terminal decline and carry out the revitalization of civilization under authoritarian rule (Coogan 1999). Despite tirelessly networking with leading European fascist groups, publishing his magnum opus of neo-fascism, *Imperium* (1948), soon followed by the manifesto based on it, *The Proclamation of London* (1949), and although he founded his own groupuscule, the European Liberation Front in 1949, Yockey's fascist international remained yet another palingenetic fantasy. Certainly, the Ku Klux Klan, Christian Identity, Odinism, Third Positionism, and a host of national Bolshevist and national revolutionary groupuscules (Lee 1999: 320–9) have operated internationally or formed clones in any society with an accommodating extreme right subculture. In practical terms, however, they have generally remained invisible to the general public and utterly impotent to affect the status quo.

Yet, the bid to globalize fascism so as to counter economic and humanistic globalization in the spirit of Yockey lives on. In September 2015, the SOVA Center, a Russian far-right monitoring organization, published the invitation of a new ultranationalist group, the World National-Conservative Movement (WNCM), to fifty-eight neo-fascist groupings worldwide in another attempt to create an effective fascist international (Shekhovtsov 2015). This was yet another sign of groupuscular neo-fascism's irrepressible creativity and ambition, which flies in the face of its objective impotence and acute marginalization. In December 2015, the ultra-right Vanguard News Network announced on its site that forty-four parties, organizations, groups and individuals based mostly in Europe and the US had participated in WNCM's internet conference. It concluded with the adoption of 'a manifesto, program and statutes that govern how the movement works', as well as forming 'a number of committees to work on various issues such as ideology, information, demonstrations, legal, military and volunteer activities and humanitarian work [sic!]'.[1] This event, however major in the mind of globalizing fascists, again passed through current affairs like a ghostly photon, undetected except by avid extremism watchers.

The glaring exception to the low-profile existence enjoyed by international neo-fascism has been neo-Nazism. Having shed its nationalist identity for a white supremacist one, and rebranding Hitler as the saviour not of Germany but of the whole Aryan race, neo-Nazism's coming of age as a universal neo-fascist movement was symbolically marked in 1962, long before the age of the internet, by the foundation by British neo-Nazis of WUNS, the World Union of National Socialists (Jackson 2017). Within a decade, neo-Nazism had also started developing its own international youth subculture, with a distinctive 'skin-head' style of dress and physical appearance (Dobratz 1997), which by the mid-1970s had appropriated elements of punk and heavy metal to create its own lucrative brand of hard rock, white power music, or white noise (Lowles and Silver 1998; Shekhovtsov 2012). Such a radical and influential departure from the narrow nationalism of Nazism in the 1930s deserves its own concept: Universal Nazism.

It was in the context of the internationalization of Nazism that William Pearce's novel *The Turner Diaries* (1978) achieved such remarkable resonance, setting white supremacism in a broad historical and geographical context and predicting a final conflict, a racial Armageddon, between the white elect and the rest of the world in apocalyptic terms so graphic that the last chapter has become the racist believer's equivalent of the Book of Revelation in the Bible. Neo-Nazism has also spawned other intensely sacralized forms of its vision of universal salvation from decadence such as the Church of the Creator and, more recently, Creativity, in which Aryanism has been explicitly turned into a New Religious Movement. It also serves as the 'go-to' form of racist extremism anywhere in the world, and not only for disaffected youth asserting their white identity. Paradoxically, the iconography of Universal Nazism has even on occasion provided the inspiration for non-whites defending their racial purity against perceived threats, as in the anti-Semitic and anti-Arab National Socialist Turkish Party or the virulently anti-Chinese Mongolian groupuscule Tsagaan Khas.

Cyberfascism, metapoliticization, Historical Revisionism

But there are a series of developments within the ideological rationale and propaganda strategy of neo-fascism which are perhaps even more profoundly innovative with respect to interwar fascism than its feigned democratization to become a conventional party-political force, its internationalization to form a worldwide groupuscular entity, or its globalization of a German racist creed. These are its virtualization into cyberfascism; its metapoliticization into 'cultural fascism'; and the creation of neo-fascism's own 'revisionist' school of modern history.

WNCM's online conference organized by Russian hosts in 2015 highlights one of the most conspicuously original aspects of neo-fascism: the trend since the rise of the internet for the highly physical, uniformed movements familiar from the 'fascist era', made up of regimented and often uniformed human beings functioning in real time in three-dimensional space, to be substituted by organizations that operate almost exclusively in cyberspace with minimal physical existence. The longevity of web-based organizations is by its nature extraordinarily unpredictable, but in 2017 the three anglo-phone ones particularly worth noting were Stormfront, the Daily Stormer and Metapedia. Such is the ephemerality and volatility of cyberfascism, readers are urged to use this intro-ductory section as a starting point to explore the current presence of disparate neo-fascisms in their own national and international cyberspace, with particular attention to hyperlinks to other fascist or right-wing phenomena, whether virtual, groupuscular, party-political or activist.

Stormfront originally grew out of a 1990s Ku Klux Klan bulletin board to become one of the oldest, best established and most sophisticated websites available to stoke the flames of white supremacist hatred and utopianism. For example, on its home page in 2017, it was careful to present itself defensively in the exclusivist discourse not of racial hatred or white supremacy but of the populist radical right: 'We are a community of racial realists and idealists. We are White Nationalists who support *true* diversity and a homeland for *all* peoples.' It then makes clear its true agenda, though still defensively: 'Thousands of organizations promote the interests, values and heritage of non-White minorities. We promote ours.' Underneath it provides links to affiliated Stormfronts in fifteen other countries and offers its visitors many pages of white supremacist material on a wide range of topics and news items, as well as the chance to take part in discussion forums.

The Daily Stormer, whose name deliberately evokes the Nazi anti-Semitic paper *Der Stürmer*, was formed in 2013 to serve the US neo-fascist alt-right movement which came to media prominence in 2016 for its endorsement of Donald Trump. A symptom of the growing sophistication of cyber-fascism is the site's use of the 'imageboard' website '4chan' to disseminate 'internet memes' among a new generation for whom social media has extensively replaced three-dimensional material reality. Even more striking in the far right's ambition and determination to fight liberal humanism in cyberspace is the creation of a neo-fascist alternative to Wikipedia, Metapedia. It originated in 2006 to provide the Swedish far right with an alternative to the 'biased' humanistic knowledge disseminated by Wikipedia, and now has versions in Hungarian, German, English, Spanish, Swedish, Romanian, Estonian, French, Greek and Slovak (Arnstad 2015). Intriguingly, Metapedia's brief article on interwar fascism corroborates the definitional role that palingenetic myth plays in its ideology, and hence the value of the empathetic approach to studying it, when it states that its core belief was that 'the European race and civilisation was [sic] in a process of catastrophic decline (such as [sic] through the effects of harmful ideologies and dysgenics) and could only be regenerated through revolutionary changes and heroism' (Metapedia 2017).

Even before the internet age and the technical possibility of 'the free movement of fascist ideas', neo-fascism had undergone a different, more intellectually high-brow sort of virtualization with the emergence of the Nouvelle Droite, or what came to be known, once it spread from France, as the European New Right (ENR) (Sunic 2012; O'Meara 2013). It was inspired by Alain de Benoist's conscious decision in the 1960s to move away from the discourse of racial superiority and revolutionary violence towards a cultural rebirth, or, rather, a national and European renaissance (de Benoist and Champetier 2012), as the solution to the prevailing climate of terminal decadence. Following Gramsci's theory of 'cultural hegemony' as the precondition of political hegemony, the New Right promulgates a 'right-wing Gramscism'. Decoded, this means that postwar fascists (though the ideologues of the ENR are at pains not to refer to themselves as such) should no longer dedicate themselves to the defeat of pluralistic liberal democracy through paramilitary violence or political engagement. Instead, they should devote their energies to a sustained campaign of *meta*politics. This means operating outside the arena of party-political life in order to concentrate on using intellectual and artistic production to overcome the forces of materialism and the degenerative ethnic and cultural 'panmixie' (miscegenation) and general spiritual chaos of modernity. The ultimate aim is to preserve diversity and ethnic and cultural 'difference' so that a new form of politics will arise to defend them.

This 'ethnopluralism' in practice creates a new form of xenophobia and 'fear of the Other', namely 'differentialist racism' (Lentin 2000), camouflaged under layers of sophisticated doublespeak. It insists on the 'human right' to belong to a distinctive, historically rooted culture (mythically conceived as ideally homogeneous and 'pure'), one which is uncontaminated by the mass migration and globalization encouraged by the liberal democratic commitment to pluralism – democracy is portrayed as 'a new totalitarianism' which promotes 'cultural genocide'. The two main intellectual precursors of metapolitical neo-fascism are the racist Italian Fascist and Eurofascist Julius Evola and the German Armin Mohler, whom we met earlier as the compiler of a highly influential compendium of (German) sources of a new postwar 'Conservative Revolution' (Griffin 2000b). The Nouvelle Droite/French New Right has had a demonstrable influence on the successful transformation of the Front National into a populist (radical) right party and thus, indirectly, to the rise of populist and identitarian right-wing politics all over the world. There were suggestions that Steve Bannon, who was briefly Donald Trump's chief strategist in 2017, is an admirer of Julius Evola's fascist 'Traditionalism' (Horowitz 2017), but it is in Russia that New Right neo-fascism has had the greatest overt impact on official politics. Under Putin it has reinforced geopolitical notions of preserving Russia's cultural homogeneity and hegemony from Europeanization thanks to the prolific publicist energies of Aleksandr Dugin, whose mission for two decades has been to revitalize Eurasianism in the mould of the Conservative Revolution (Shekthovtsov 2008b).

A year after Alain de Benoist published the seminal text of the revision of fascism in a metapolitical direction, *Vu de droite* [Seen from the Right], in 1977, the Institute for Historical Review had been set up in the US to dedicate itself to another 'metapolitical' tactic to make fascist ideas of rebirth more acceptable, this time by calling into doubt not just the link between Nazism and the Holocaust but the very fact that the Nazis set about committing systematic genocide against the Jewish people. In the institute's many publications dedicated to 'negationism', whether the persecution of racial enemies, Holocaust denial, minimizing the war crimes of the Third Reich or highlighting those of the Allies, the academic discourse and scholarly apparatus of professional historians is deployed – sometimes with considerable sophistication – to create a counter-narrative to the factual history of the *Shoah*. (In the US, Jonah Goldberg (2008) used a similar technique to convince Republican readers that fascism has left-wing roots that still informs the Democratic tradition of state intervention in social issues.)

In its books and journals, international Historical Revisionism has maintained a barrage of what can now be called 'alternative facts' to convince anti-fascists or reassure fellow apologists for Nazism of a number of propositions: there was no deliberate campaign by the Third Reich to commit genocide against Jews; extermination camps never existed; the gas chambers really were shower rooms; the massacre of Jews in the East by the special squads of the SS Einsatzkommandos is a propaganda lie; Hitler never gave an order to exterminate Jews; proportionally no more Jews died as a result of the war (no more than 600,000!) than any other ethnic group or social category; the emaciated corpses found in the death camps were the result of US bombardments that interrupted food supplies; Jews have invented the elaborate 'hoax' of the *Shoah* to justify the creation of the state of Israel; in any case, mass murder of Jews was one of many genocides in history and should not be allowed to monopolize memories of the war; the Allies committed more war crimes than the Nazis, and so on (Lipstadt 1993; Evans 2002). However, Revisionism has proved much more effective in salving the consciences of fascists and (to use a biblical expression) searing them against collective guilt than in convincing anti-fascists of Nazism's innocence.

In the West, negationism (which has an important Islamic variant) can be practised at many different levels of sophistication. Many Universal Nazis see Holocaust denial as part of their campaign to perpetuate the Third Reich's campaign against the Jews, but also as a way of calling into question the credibility of anti-fascist arguments, presenting Nazism as a heroic attempt to prevent the ethnic peoples of Western civilization from committing suicide by falling into a black hole of multiculturalism, materialism, globalization and Americanization. Students of fascism reading this book are urged to see their commitment to scientific methodology in studying fascism as vital to maintaining the humanistic counter-offensive to Historical Revisionism and all other attempts to manipulate academic discourse and methodology to vindicate racial or cultural supremacism and the inhumanity that flows from it.

Terrorist neo-fascism

We have already touched on perhaps the most disturbing innovation within the development of neo-fascism, namely the recourse to terrorist violence in the lone-wolf spirit of 'leaderless resistance', without orders from above. (Of course, 'terrorism' is a value-laden word, but in the context of fascist attempts to realize fantasies of a reborn ultra-nation through extreme violence it can hopefully be used uncontentiously for most readers.) Here again we are dealing with a component that before 1945 was a recurrent trait of the more aggressive fascist movements. Paramilitary groups in the 'fascist epoch' used violence to target ideological and racial enemies and to intimidate opponents, and several movements would probably have instituted a terror apparatus on Nazi lines had they been in power to enforce the 'new order' and purge the nation of 'decadence' (Law 2016). Fascist *squadristi*, the Nazi SA (Gellately 1991) and the Legionary hit-squads (Clark 2012), as well as the Croatian Ustasha Militia (Tomasevich 2001), often dedicated themselves to their punitive expeditions and local campaigns of intimidation with chilling gusto. Here too an integrated trait of interwar fascism has split off to become an autonomous, specialized form of neo-fascist activism. At its ideological core, fascism contains the potential for the cult of cathartic and transformative violence, following the logic of 'creative destruction' that flows from its imperative to carry out a revolution against the existing decadent order (Forgacs 1994; Albanese and del Hierrero 2016); however, it is not movements but individuals that now carry out the most destructive acts.

There has always been an uninterrupted tradition of low-level, localized fascist violence which could loosely be seen as 'terroristic' whenever it has the primary aim of striking fear in a whole category of human beings (Jews, migrants, communists, ethnic minorities, gays, drug-addicts, etc.) and force it out of the neighbourhood or the country. In this sense, the Ku Klux Klan, with its cross burnings and lynchings by masked men, can be seen as forerunners of modern racist terrorism, though it lacked the revolutionary myth to qualify as neo-fascist until it started actively collaborating with neo-Nazism at the Aryan fests first organized in the late 1980s. At this point its white supremacism entered into symbiosis with the palingenetic myth of Universal Nazis that the whole world is to be purged of non-Aryan blood. The UK saw the formation in 1992 of Combat 18, one of the first groupuscules dedicated exclusively to fascist violence in the name of Adolf Hitler (whose initials are alluded to in the two digits of 18). It has branches in several European countries and ties to violent far-right groups in the US. More recently, National Action surfaced as another British group dedicated to terroristic violence, only to be banned in 2016. Both have counterparts wherever Universal Nazism and ultra-nationalism have developed a significant extreme right-wing subculture, as in Russia – groupuscules such as the RONA, the RFO 'Memory' and the Russian Right Party – many of them ephemeral, but still important in maintaining the physically threatening presence of a fascist cultic milieu (Verkhovsky 2016).

Just how simplistic it would be to reduce all fascist terrorist violence to 'neo-Nazism' was underlined when Matthew Heimbach, the organizer of the 'Unite the Right' rally in Charlottesville in August 2017, which culminated in a terrorist attack on anti-fascist protestors, chose to wear a

T-shirt for the occasion celebrating not Hitler but Cornelius Codreanu, leader of the Romanian Iron Guard. When he appeared with other members of the alt-right to support Donald Trump at the Republican National Convention in July 2016, he had also expressed his admiration for José Antonio (of the Spanish Falange), Oswald Mosley (the British Union of Fascists) and Léon Degrelle (the Belgian Rexist Party), as well as Bashar al-Assad, Saddam Hussein and Colonel Muammar Gaddafi. It is also worth noting that, in the US, an important contributor to white supremacism is a sect-like movement based on a highly unorthodox and racist variant of fundamentalist Christianity, Christian Identity (CI).

Though CI in theory should oppose the paganism of Nazism, in practice many of its militants readily join forces with Nazis in attacking common enemies, and its anti-Semitism, along with neo-Nazism, was an important influence on David Copeland, the London nail-bomber (McLagen and Lowles 2000). Similarly, contemporary Ku Klux Klan members may still swear allegiance to a racist form of Protestantism but have no scruples about attending Aryan fests with members of the Church of the Creator, for whom the white race has replaced Christ. The political career of Tom Metzger, the leader of the overtly terroristic White Aryan Resistance, reveals the porous membrane that exists between racist Christianity and neo-Nazi paganism in contemporary America, as graphically illustrated by the 1991 documentary *Blood in the Face* by Anne Bohlen, Kevin Rafferty and James Ridgeway.

The discovery by German authorities in 2011 that the secret National Socialist Underground had for over a decade been committing a series of bank robberies and murders of Muslims (so-called Kebab Murders) underlines the continuing potential for neo-fascism groupuscules to adopt the strategy of a 'spontaneist' terrorist war against society, albeit enacted by minute cells of combatants. Their acts should be seen against the background of the 1,485 violent crimes with a far-right motivation recorded in 2015 in Germany alone at the height of anti-immigrant protests, few of which will have involved the premeditated actions of centrally organized groups (Koehler 2016). In 2017 the database on right-wing terrorism maintained by the German Institute of Radicalization and de-Radicalization Studies held information on a disturbing list of neo-fascist activities in the Federal Republic, including '92 right-wing terrorist actors (groups and individuals that could be identified since 1963); 123 right-wing terrorist incidents using explosives since 1971 (including successful and failed attempts); 2,173 right-wing arson attacks since 1971; 229 cases of murder with a right-wing background since 1971' (GIRDS 2017). Compared with the quantity of crimes committed by the National Socialism between 1919 and 1945, such numbers fade into insignificance. However, the ability of minute shards of the total palingenetic vision of interwar Nazism still to motivate disaffected groups to continue to inflict death, misery and fear on an intimate, local scale is not to be forgotten, and behind each of these statistics lies another lost or shattered life. On occasion, neo-fascist terrorism can take on more substantial, ideologically elaborated forms as a sustained war on 'the system'.

The most deadly and prolonged collective campaign of neo-fascist or 'black terrorism' to date was inflicted on Italy between 1969 and 1980, the so-called Years of Lead. The phrase refers to a period of major dislocation in public, university and political life deliberately fomented by the revolutionary left in random acts of terrorism carried out by the Red Brigades against the 'system' and by the revolutionary right in the so-called Strategy of Tension which aimed to bring about a right-wing coup. This involved the direct collusion of formations such as Nuclei Armati Rivoluzionari, Ordine Nuovo, Avanguardia Nazionale, Ordine Nero, Terza Posizione and a host of even smaller groupuscules, many of them inspired by Julius Evola, with elements from within the government, police and judiciary. In the event, neo-fascism proved far too marginalized and out of step with the pro-democratic mood of the times to pose a credible threat to the structures of the state, but for over a decade it had succeeded in fuelling a permanent sense of national crisis (Ferraresi 1996; Albanese and del Hierrero 2016: 137–58).

The failure of every other permutation of postwar fascism to break out of its ghettoization or complete the first steps towards realizing its utopia, however deep the national crisis, left one final, desperate outlet for revolutionary nationalism: the (so-called) lone-wolf terrorist attack. Based on a tactic already adopted in the past by anarchists, communists, separatists, resistance fighters, religious fundamentalists, anti-abortionists and eco-terrorists, an individual fanatically committed to saving his or her imagined ultra-nation from decadence would attack a symbol of the hated liberal multicultural 'system', acting largely independently of a movement or groupuscule. The most lethal and notorious single act of terrorist violence to date by Germany's neo-Nazi right was the bombing of the Munich Oktoberfest in 1980, when thirteen people were killed and 225 injured by the rightwing extremist Gundolf Köhler. Since then, both Europe and the US have seen sporadic lone-wolf attacks on various living symbols of the threat posed to 'Aryan civilization' (e.g. a multi-race family,[2] a Muslim returning from prayer,[3] African Americans,[4] an MP favouring immigration[5] and the Holocaust Museum in Washington).[6]

Before 2017, two attacks in particular, those of Timothy McVeigh and Anders Breivik, had demonstrated the extraordinary capacity of the new ideological and technical resources available to neo-fascists to enable a fanatic to execute practically single-handed deadly (and utterly futile) acts of destruction against what are, for the killer, living symbols of what is corrupting and undermining the idealized ultranation of their imagination. As in so much modern terrorism, citizens innocently living out their own normality had been transformed and dehumanized by the politicized palingenetic mindset into 'demonized Others', their murder intended to 'awaken' society to a deeper truth about the world, or at least undermine its sense of security and self-belief. What in the 1930s was attempted by members of the paramilitary units of mass movements could now be undertaken by a single individual radicalized by neo-fascism's cultic milieu.

To study the deeper motivations of McVeigh's attack on the Alfred P. Murrah Federal Building in Oklahoma, which took 168 lives and injured 680 more (Michel and Herbeck 2001), and Breivik's successful planting of a van bomb in the government quarter of Oslo followed by the execution of 69 members of the Worker's Youth League on the island of Utøya (Seierstad 2015) is to realize just how idiosyncratic, complex and curiously *private* and *socially isolated* the mind of contemporary neo-fascists can be. Not only is there no need for them to be an official member of a hierarchical movement whose ideological rationales for violence emanate from a charismatic leader or a specialized party department; their subjective analysis of history and the need for revolutionary action to save the mythicized ultra-nation is no longer synchronized with the objective state of the world. They can thus enter a fanatical state of mind, a kind of self-induced psychosis (medical psychosis is rarely involved) fixated on the destruction of symbolic targets, but without any capacity to evaluate realistically the rationality of their goals and the outcome of their actions, their humanistic values transcended by the higher moral demands of the 'cause'.

Living in self-imposed seclusion for years, Breivik used the luxury of the internet, which provides information without any of the constraints of academic rigour, to create an elaborate ideological rationale for his plot to 'save' Norway from Islamization in the form of an alternative history, cut and pasted from websites, of Islam's secular war against Christian Europe. The result was *2083: A Declaration of European Independence*, a sprawling but valuable document of the solitary neo-fascist mindset at work in an age where new issues, new technologies, new forms of communication, and new possibilities of waging war on society have arisen which were inconceivable in the 'fascist epoch'.

Breivik's fantasy 'ultra-nation', which shifts between Norway, Europe and the West, and the rationales of Aryanism, cultural Christianity and the kitsch warrior ethos encountered in video-games such as *Assassin's Creed*, is the figment of a mind utterly disconnected from reality in its desperation to endow life with a higher, sacred purpose (Griffin 2012b). The murders he so carefully planned and trained himself to commit by playing hours of *World of Warcraft* were supposed to trigger a process of national awakening that would lead to Europe's rebirth as a homogeneous, existentially secure, 'culturally' Christian society, worthy of its heroic past and purged of foreign contamination. What they inspired instead was the creation of a vast memorial shrine of cut flowers which formed outside Oslo Cathedral as individuals spontaneously paid a tribute to the victims.

Neo-fascists: out of step with the present, but still determined to 'make' history

For convinced fascists, the 1930s must have seemed a blessed time when their palingenetic hopes for national rebirth appeared, in the words of Seamus Heaney's poem 'The Cure at Troy', rhymed with history, an epiphanic state the Irish poet William Butler Yeats himself recorded at a time when he too had been temporally seduced by the sense of participating in a historical sea-change through his support for fascism (Cullingford 1981: 75).

Since 1945 the powerful tides of a new era have smashed every new rhyming scheme that fascism could invent to smithereens. Nevertheless, there will continue to be those whose quest for transcendent meaning and agency makes them susceptible to the vision of a new day dawning for civilization, even if it is seen through the distorting lenses of nation, race and hatred. Every fresh act of neo-fascist violence, every event designed to stir up memories of the fascist epoch, every reference to ethnic cultures as organic entities with their own political rights and destinies, is a reminder of the need for the human sciences not to close the file on neo-fascism or treat it as a footnote to the fascist epoch.

6
Conclusion: Fascism, Post-Fascism and Post *Fascism*

Four guiding principles for the productive use of the term 'fascism'

Just as the 'new wave' of fascist studies was gaining momentum, Umberto Eco, the famous Italian intellectual novelist who had experienced Italian Fascism first hand, published what is now regarded as a classic article identifying fourteen 'common features' of what he called 'Eternal' or 'Ur-fascism' (Eco 1995). Intriguingly, none of the features corresponds to the definition that has informed this book, and every one of them can be found in a variety of political movements or regimes which according to this book are *not* fascist. This sobering fact once again underlines a point that should never be forgotten when working in this area, namely the contentious nature of 'fascism' as a term. To parody a famous observation in Bernard Shaw's *Pygmalion*, 'It is impossible for an expert on fascism to open his [or her!] mouth without making some other expert hate or despise him.'

For the sake of clarity, I propose to round off this inevitably personal introduction to fascism as a key subject in political theory by offering a number of guiding principles for the study of fascism (though the fourth has five sub-clauses!). They hopefully serve to summarize the book's main argument about its nature and status as a generic concept used in historical and political science and to highlight the difference between its connotations before and after 1945. I conclude with some advice about avoiding arid definitional arguments and theoretical disputes and some suggestions both about where comparative fascist studies are going and how students and researchers can contribute to their further maturing and progress.

1 *The ideal type*: There can be no objective, purely empirical, uncontentious definition of 'fascism' (see chapter 1, note 1). This is because any definition of a generic term in the human sciences is at bottom an *ideal type* (see chapter 1, note 2), an artificial construct that acts as a taxonomic (classificatory) and heuristic (investigatory) device to allow segments of historical and socio-political reality to be identified and researched comparatively by reference to a generic concept (in this case 'fascism'). As such they can be understood or investigated as permutations of a general pattern of phenomenon, or, to use biological metaphors, species of the same genus, or linked by 'family resemblance' (see chapter 1, note 2) *while not denying the uniqueness of each of its specimens*. It is an optical illusion caused by language, or an epistemological fallacy (a misunderstanding of the relationship between concepts and reality and how we 'know' the world), that fascism is a 'real' entity that can be described on the basis of 'self-evident' traits, that it has an essence to be objectively identified, or that it is an animate historical and social actor that has qualities of a biological organism which grows or declines or acts.

2 *The empathetic paradigm*: To avoid methodological naivety, new research into fascism should be informed by at least some awareness of the existence of long 'Marxist' and 'liberal' traditions of engaging with generic fascism and of the tangled and often cantankerous historical debate about its meaning; however, it should not get bogged down in this debate. At the very least, it should show familiarity with what has been called in this book the 'empathetic approach' to defining fascism as a form of politics, which has gained ever wider acceptance and application among researchers since the 1990s. If

an idiosyncratic 'new' concept of fascism is applied to research, then for the sake of academic integrity its main points of convergence and divergence with respect to mainstream Marxist and liberal theory and the heuristic 'added value' it brings should be made clear, so that the growing community of academics working in comparative fascist studies can more easily integrate it into their work.

3 *The empirical basis of the empathetic ideal type*: This ideal type conflicts both with Marxist approaches, which reduce fascism to an agent or tool of capitalism, and with the older liberal tendency to see it as fundamentally irrational, nihilistic or undefinable. Instead it seeks to understand fascism generically in terms of how fascists themselves understood their political mission. Hence the ideal type originated initially as a result of a largely unconscious process of idealizing abstraction engaged in by a series of scholars who studied concrete episodes of the history of fascism in considerable detail while taking it *seriously* (without endorsing its values or programme) as a political force based on what was for the fascists themselves a 'positive' ideology. As such, it had its own characteristic diagnosis of the present state of the nation or contemporary history, and its own vision of the future or the ideal society to be realized through a revolutionary process of total societal transformation. Prominent among these scholars were George Mosse, Eugen Weber, Emilio Gentile, Zeev Sternhell and Stanley Payne. In the 1990s, my own contribution to refining this approach (Griffin 1991) was one of a number of publications in that period moving towards a consistent theory of fascism as a form of revolutionary ultranationalism.

The application of the ideal type to postwar phenomena associated with the extreme right has also demonstrated its empirical value in distinguishing neo-fascism from other forms of the right, in particular revolutionary from radical but still (technically) democratic populism, and from jihadist forms of Islamist politics (though there is less academic agreement in this area). One feature of the application of my variant of this ideal type is that, by highlighting the vision of ultranationalist rebirth as the ineliminable core, it reveals the kinship to interwar fascism of virtual, intellectual, 'cultural' and pseudo-academic variants of extreme right-wing activism such as cyberfascist websites, the metapolitical New Right and Historical Revisionism.

4 *The definitional components of the 'empathetic' ideal type of fascism*: Since the 1990s the empirical validation of the usefulness of this ideal type, the range of movements and primary sources embraced by the sub-discipline, and the number of scholars from different countries applying the empathetic paradigm has been constantly growing. The 'ideal type' is formulated in as many ways as there are experts prepared to define it, but the constant, 'definitional' elements of the so-called fascist minimum in the light of this book can be summarized as follows:

• *Ultranationalism*: 'Fascism' is a particular form of extreme nationalism based on a utopian concept of the nation as a healthy, powerful and heroic organic entity (termed in this book an 'ultra-nation') which a self-appointed vanguard of militant ultranationalists attempts to turn into reality, in the first instance with or without populist support, though in the long term an entire 'national community' is to be mobilized as a result of the fascist revolution, whether violent or cultural. The ultra-nation is a particular form of the 'imagined community' (Anderson 1983) which is not necessarily seen as coterminous with a historical nation or nation-state – as in the case of the 'white race' posited by Aryanism, white supremacism and Universal Nazism. Interwar Nazism, for example, already developed the vision of a national community which merged elements both of the historic German nation-state and of the supranational Nordic and Aryan race. Nor does the ultra-nation necessarily embrace such common interwar components as negative eugenics, biological racism, the terror state, corporatism or imperialism. Even the leader cult, uniformed paramilitarism and elaborate displays of political religion, so characteristic of interwar fascism, are not treated by the empathetic paradigm as definitional traits of fascism and can in any case be found in a wide variety of illiberal politics.

The ultranationalism based on the project of the reborn ultra-nation rejects liberal ideas of citizenship, multiculturalism, individualism and the equality of human rights as the basis of society, along with forms of nationalism derived from liberal ideas of citizenship, residence and acculturation (*ius soli*). Instead it promotes the concept of an affective belonging to an organic national community, whether contained within a nation-state, an imagined global ethnicity, a race or ethnically based culture, a mystic membership made possible through such anthropological ties as mythicized history, ancestry, place, language, culture and blood (*ius sanguinis*). Some fascisms see the removal or physical purging of alien or decadent elements from society as the precondition for the ultra-nation to come into being, while many do not. But all are committed to an ideology of revolutionary (palingenetic) ultranationalism tailored to the crisis conditions in which the imagined 'ultra-nation' finds itself.

- *The belief in a crisis threatening the ultra-nation*: The latent organic ultra-nation to be achieved through the fascist revolution is perceived as exposed to an urgent or sustained existential threat. This threat can be attributed to a wide range of factors determined by the prevailing historical circumstances, but it typically expresses itself in a sense of 'crisis', 'decadence' or 'degeneration': for example, military, industrial, demographic, moral or cultural decline, the production of 'degenerate' or meaningless art, anonymous townscapes and architecture, national humiliation, whether economic or military, loss of national essence and virility, loss of identity, erosion of communal cohesion, collective amnesia about a heroic past, miscegenation with racial, ideological, dysgenic or moral 'enemies', and contamination by decadent ideologies (e.g. pacifism, communism, cosmopolitanism, globalization, multiculturalism, political correctness), by alien cultures (e.g. African-American, Jewish, Slav, Islamic, experimentation, abstraction and unintelligibility in art) or by unhealthy social practices and movements (e.g. consumerism, homosexuality, feminism, mixed marriage, social media, materialism, communism). In the fascist mindset, unique combinations of such factors work together to undermine the cohesion of the national community, the heroic conception of the ultra-nation, and the possibility of achieving transcendence through national belonging.

- *Calls or plans for the total conquest of (political or cultural) power*: Some committed fascists (see p. 55) are convinced that the catastrophic situation or the creeping decadence presently threatening the organic cohesion and strength of the nation, and hence the emergence of the ultra-nation, can eventually be reversed by a violent military putsch or an electoral victory reinforced by a powerful populist movement, while the New Right works towards a gradual cultural revolution winning hegemony for ultranationalist values and the rejection of multiculturalism, which will in turn bring about a political transformation. All these processes are supposed to lead in time to a national 'reawakening' and totalizing rebirth in all spheres. In practice, the fascist conquest of the state in Italy and Germany was the result of a democratic process backed up by the intimidating use of paramilitary power. As for Croatia's seizure of power in order to carry out an ethnic revolution, this was possible only because of an exceptional situation created temporarily by the Axis occupation of the Balkans.

Since the war, when political space for fascist movements shrank and the critical social mass to produce charismatic leaders or carry out a successful coup failed to materialize, fascism has changed radically to adapt. The resulting 'neo-fascism' has assumed many forms and deployed a number of different strategies to gain power, ranging from carrying out a military coup, to winning democratic elections, to changing cultural hegemony in favour of fascist ideals, to the use of terrorist violence to spark a race war or awaken the ultra-nation, to simply using cyberspace to keep alive the fascist dream and maintain the faith until, at some point in the future, historical conditions favour the emergence of a new national or civilizational order. With the decline of the nation-state and the globalization of so many phenomena, it is increasingly frequent for the fascist 'new order' and the regeneration of the ultra-nation to be conceived in international and transnational terms of European or Western renewal as a whole and to resort to worldwide cyberfascism and metapolitical, supranational cultural initiatives.

• *The goal of creating a fascist (and neo-fascist) new order*: In the interwar period, the reversal of decadence is generally conceived in archetypal mythic terms as a total and imminent phoenix-like rebirth, a process of renewal, regeneration, a new dawn, a new beginning. This palingenesis will usher in a new phase of national greatness drawing on the hidden resources of what is conceived as an immortal and invisible ultra-nation founded on primordial, eternal values, and in some cases (though not all) on the 'purity' of a superior race (which geographically may or not be coterminous with a nation-state). In other words, where possible fascists instinctively operate what theorists of nationalism call a 'primordialist' concept of the nation, as epitomized in the Nazi concept of the Germans as an 'Aryan race', the Fascist cult of *romanità*, and the Turanian myth of the origins of the Magyar cultivated by Hungarism. The world was forced to witness the catastrophic results of fascist attempts to realize their organic new order.

In the postwar era, though palingenetic myth is still definitional within our ideal type, the timetable for the rebirth and the entity to be reborn, what constitutes the ultra-nation, has become far more nebulous and ill-defined for many fascists. The rebirth of the ultra-nation from within the nation-state is still generally assumed to be integral to a process of regeneration affecting Western civilization as a whole and ushering in a sea-change in world history. But neo-fascism is characterized by so many palingenetic visions and schemes that it is impossible to generalize about how this rebirth will occur, especially now that, for many fascists, the rebirth has been indefinitely postponed and must wait for the collapse of liberal civilization from within – what Julius Evola (1961) calls 'riding the tiger'. The process of society's renewal is hence rarely described in any detail. Thus, the account of the racial apocalypse at the end of *The Turner Diaries* (Pearce [1978] 2013) refers to a 'cleansing hurricane' which will purge the world of dysgenic human life, but the new Aryan world that will arise is not portrayed, any more than what will occur after the 'Conservative Revolution' longed for by Armin Mohler (1950). For most neo-fascists, notably the several thousand militant Universal Nazis in the world and a handful of terrorists determined to rid the country of multiculturalism, Islamization and mass migration, the struggle against the decadence of the system in the name of higher ultranationalist values has become an end in itself. It is pursued using very different analyses and tactics, but – in stark contrast to the interwar Europe when the threat of revolutionary violence was very real – most fascist imagining is cut off from reality, and even the fantasies of attacks on the system in which neo-fascists indulge mostly remain virtual.

- *A modern(ist) vision of the fascist new order which embraces elements of a mythicized past*: The new order, however and whenever conceived, even in the case of futurist Fascism in Italy, draws its vital (mythic) strength from the 'usable past' of the ultra-nation (nation, civilization or race). It is thus a misconception to assume the fascist quest for rootedness and concern with the past is somehow reactionary or anti-modern. On the contrary, fascism is a dynamic, future-oriented and (would-be) future-conquering ideology, which sees itself as constituting an alternative and viable modernity to a decadent present. It strives for a 'rooted modernity' and can even be conceived as a form of modernism in itself (Griffin 2007).

Catching the fish without being entangled in the net

It has been stressed throughout this book that what distinguishes different ideal types of fascism is their *usefulness* (their heuristic value) when applied to concrete research questions. Moreover, it should be remembered that human reality abounds in phenomena to which several different and only partially overlapping ideal types can be applied. Nazism, for example, can be seen both as unique and, simultaneously, as a form of fascism, totalitarianism, political religion, political modernism, paranoid politics or autocratic patriarchy – and doubtless other generic concepts can be applied to it. Any ideal type should be thus treated pragmatically as *a* potential key and not as *the* key to a debate, and applied intelligently, not mechanically and uncritically.

Since ideal types create an artificial taxonomic (classificatory) tidiness in a debate, students should not be disconcerted if they encounter apparently conflicting ideological components within the 'same' fascist movement. Italian Fascism, for example, was a plural phenomenon, containing many rival theories, and even philosophies, of what the new state should be, as well as conservative and futuristic, elitist and populist, bourgeois and working-class, urban and rural, youthful and gerontocratic, revolutionary and reactionary currents. As we have stressed (in chapter 3), it was also contributed to professionally by many Italians who, deep down, did not believe in the Fascist vision at all but still were actively part of fascism. Like all fascisms (and all political systems of whatever ideological justification), Fascism was intrinsically a 'messy mixture' (Roberts 2000), which embraced elements such as ultra-conservative Catholicism that contradicted the pagan cult of *romanità*, which in turn was in direct conflict both with technocratic and futurist visions of the new Italy and with Giovanni Gentile's Hegelian theory of the ethical state, which formed the basis of the official definition of Fascist ideology in the *Enciclopedia Italiana*.

The practical implication of such ideological 'messiness' for writing lucid and coherent student projects relating to fascism is clear. Unless definitional, methodological or generic issues are at the centre of an essay or dissertation project, as students embarking on a topic which demands a working definition of fascism you are recommended

1 to demonstrate that you are aware that it is a contested term;
2 to select or formulate a version of the paradigmatic definition presented in this volume, or, if you have become

convinced by another theory or an approach which rejects the need for formulating definitions altogether (e.g. Passmore 2002), to introduce it, explaining why it is preferable to apply it in the present context;

3 to move on with as smooth a transition as possible to answering the question in a fully referenced and empirically corroborated argument, namely by focusing on those segments of historical or contemporary realities illuminated by the ideal type that has been introduced.

In this you should be guided by a passion for the extraordinary individuality and uniqueness of fascist phenomena, rather than their genericness, and be fascinated by the singular human stories and sequences of (often terrible) events that acquire an extra dimension once they are placed in their full historical context and understood through the lens of the empathetic ideal type we have presented.

The Chinese philosopher Zhuang Zhu (fourth century BC) said it better:

> The fish trap exists because of the fish. Once you've got the fish you can forget the trap. The rabbit snare exists because of the rabbit. Once you've got the rabbit, you can forget the snare. Words exist because of meaning. Once you've got the meaning, you can forget the words. Where can I find a man who has forgotten words so I can talk with him?

So perhaps there is a fifth principle suggested by this book. Once you find yourself engaging with fascism as a living historical, political and human reality, forget about the theory of palingenetic ultranationalism that helped lead you to this point. The ideal type of fascism offered here should be seen as a trap to catch slippery human realities which would otherwise be less intelligible but should not be allowed to become another sort of trap, one which hinders engagement with empirical reality and acts as an obstacle to collaborative communication with colleagues, rather than facilitating them. And remember that, as Brecht insisted, 'THE TRUTH IS CONCRETE'. The academic or analytic truth you seek to establish in your essays should also be as concrete in empirical and human terms as possible.

Post *Fascism*: What you can get out of comparative fascist studies

If you have reached this point in the text after reading this book (i.e. post *Fascism*) you may well be having doubts about whether, given its intrinsic contentiousness and complexity, it might not be better to move on to another specialist area of the humanities (not that another area would not have its own complexities!). If so, I ask you to consider the following points.

In terms of what fascist studies can do for students as a topic in the human sciences, they certainly provide a terrain on which to develop or refine many skills essential to professional work that involves a superior research ability. They demand a combination of historiography with advanced conceptual and methodological sophistication and involve events whose explanations often break down artificial barriers between political, sociological, anthropological and psychological approaches. Fascist studies are like an assault course in expert research techniques.

Beyond this, fascist studies can act as a portal which opens into a deeper understanding of many movements in past or contemporary history that involve such fanatical devotion to a revolutionary cause that they are responsible for extreme acts of violence and barbarity, as in the Bolshevik, Maoist, Pol Pot and IS states in the last century. They also provide good training for understanding the abuse of state power in the name of an organically, nebulously and mythically conceived 'people', whose moral well-being is held to supersede individual human rights, such as the right not to be tortured, not to be executed, not to be held without due legal process, and not to be persecuted on ethnic or religious grounds. Such examples underline the *humanistic* and *humanizing* value of studying phenomena that involve or lead to calculated acts of inhumanity and reinforce the status of history and political studies as disciplines integral to the humanities.

Contributing to the next phase in fascist studies

My final reflections are directed to those who have consulted the present volume at a postgraduate level and feel motivated to enrich the discipline of comparative fascist studies through their choice of topic and subsequent research. If you focus not on what fascist studies can do for you but on what you as a researcher can do for comparative fascist studies, a host of fresh possibilities opens up. For one thing, given that comparative fascist studies are mostly anglophone, much work is still to be done by specialists with the appropriate linguistic skills and cultural background to add more pieces to the jigsaw puzzle of the fascist or para-fascist phenomena that arose in the interwar period in such countries as Poland, Czechoslovakia, the Slovak Republic, Bulgaria, Ukraine, the Balkan states (other than Croatia) and the Baltic states, about which so little exists in English (Costa Pinto and Kallis 2014).

Such work would be guaranteed international dissemination, especially if an effort was made to integrate the findings within comparative fascist studies by adopting the empathetic approach to basic definitional and classificatory issues, which has at least for the time being become the conceptual *lingua franca* in the field. The discipline also needs to know a lot more about the fascist component that has been detected in twentieth-century ultranationalist movements and regimes that arose in India, the Middle East (notably Lebanon), China, Japan, South Africa and Latin America (notably Argentina, Brazil and Chile) under the direct influence of European fascism, and how far the empathetic paradigm of fascism can enrich understanding of the individual phenomena in a coherent international perspective. This could lead to a far more methodologically coherent exploration of fascism as a global phenomenon than existing volumes on the topic (e.g. Larsen 2001; Wippermann 2009), which base their analysis on ideal types of fascism so idiosyncratic that they compromise their survey's value to practical research in comparative studies.

As for neo-fascism, there is a permanent need for humanistic organizations to monitor the output of revolutionary ultranationalists in print, in social media and in cyber-space, especially as regards their rallies, festivals, concerts, hate-crimes and terrorist attacks, their attempts to pose as democratic activists, and their revisionist efforts to rehabil-itate Nazism or run metapolitical campaigns to regenerate homogeneous cultures under threat from modernity, to stop 'ethnic suicide' and 'cultural genocide' being inflicted by multiculturalism and mass immigration. It could be extremely valuable for such monitoring agencies and those who work in the area of counter-extremism and counter-radicalization and the sociology of violence to enter tightly focused collab-orations with academics equipped with a sophisticated conceptual and methodological approach to generic fascism This would open the door to fruitful knowledge-sharing with equivalent collaborations in other countries grappling with the threat of the far right, and so forge international networks of the sort that already exist for counter-terrorism.

As for comparative fascist studies as a sub-discipline, there is no shortage of conferences and journals prepared to publish innovative material, but a major step towards creating a genuine sense of academic community is the foundation in 2018 of the International Association for Comparative Fascist Studies (COMFAS), based in the Central European University and formed in association with the journal *Fascism: Journal for Comparative Fascist Studies*. It aims to create both a virtual and, through its conferences and workshops, a physical forum for researchers into interwar and postwar fascism from anywhere in the world prepared to engage critically with current trends in the field and help it mature into a genuine international and multidisciplinary enterprise.

Beyond filling in the many gaps in the record and keeping the discipline up to date, there are three important trends in the evolution of fascist studies to consider when formulating an original topic and defining the related research questions and objectives. The first, pioneered by George Mosse (1974) and Emilio Gentile (1996) and sometimes known to its detractors disparagingly as 'culturalist', understands fascism as not only a political or ideological phenomenon but a cultural and social anthropological one in the widest sense (Griffin 2002, 2007). The interest is thus in fascism's relationship to the arts, architecture, philosophy, myth, ritual, cosmology, symbology, and the creation of sacred spaces, which is seen at least partly as an attempt to reverse modernity's disenchantment of the world through utopian projects that offer to its most fanatical converts meaning, purpose, transcendence, and a social and existential centre. There is much exciting work to be done to deepen understanding of how fascism offers its converts a way to re-establish a sense of roots, bearings and 'fixity' so as to withstand what Zygmunt Bauman (2000) called 'liquid modernity' and George Mosse 'the rush of time' (Griffin 2004). Typical of what might be called this 'anthropological turn' (to distinguish it from a 'cultural turn') are studies exploring the cult of the body (Mangan 2000), the new man (Sandulescu 2004; Feldman et al. 2017), a new Nazi conscience (Koonz 2005), a new morality that even licenses genocide (Kallis 2008), the relationship of fascism to time (Esposito 2015a), technocratic myth (Esposito 2015b), modernism (Griffin 2007, 2017), and the architectural and town-planning quest for a sacred centre (Kallis 2014). This burgeoning area of fascist studies creates the mental space for a stream of research topics where cultural undertakings and the production of artefacts assume a new significance within such concepts as 'revolutionary nationalism' and 'rooted modernism'.

Deeply bound up with the New Wave is the call for fascism not to be treated as a monolithic, self-contained, almost 'pure' political entity simply existing alongside and largely independent from other forms of illiberal right. As David Roberts argues persuasively in *Fascist Interactions: Proposals for a New Approach to Fascism and its Era* (2016), it is precisely fascism's fissiparous, factious and promiscuous nature, as well as the intense pragmatism of its drive to power at all costs, that predisposes it so powerfully towards transnational entanglements, borrowings from foreign role models and hybridization. It thus needs to be studied not in isolation but in its interactions, both with the national conservative right and with the new, highly dynamic forms of right that emerged in many parts of the Westernized world after 1918. Greater understanding of each fascism's unique cultural embeddedness, trajectory and entanglements in each country should make it possible to establish eventually what

Roberts calls 'the braided dynamic encompassing the web of interaction' which constituted 'a new universe on the Right' (2016: 224) of which fascism was only a 'subset' (2016: 227). Young researchers are encouraged to contemplate contributing to this new direction in comparative research, which breaks fascism out of its present isolation from its wider political environment.

A third new development that is rich in potential topics for those contemplating doctoral research relates to its previously largely neglected transnational dimension. Michael Ledeen (1972) wrote a pioneering work on the attempts to create a fascist international, and Herzstein (1982) pieced together fascinating glimpses into the Nazi plans for Europe after the Third Reich's final victory. I tried to take stock of pan-European fascist initiatives before and after the war (Griffin 2008), while the world of international neo-fascism was opened up by Kevin Coogan's investigation (1999) of Francis Yockey's postwar attempts to bring about a fascist international. But now that the heuristic value of the empathetic paradigm of fascism has established itself sufficiently to be taken for granted, the energy that might have been wasted on debating definitions has now been liberated for a deeper engagement with neglected aspects of fascism itself. Apart from its entanglements with the non-fascist right, an area now opening up for fruitful investigation consists of the many episodes of *histoires croisées* and transnational interactions which underline the need to see at the heart of fascist imaginings not the nation-state but the ultra-nation, either in its nation-state or supranational manifestation. Pioneering works in this direction have already appeared in an in-depth comparative study of the paramilitary formations of Fascism and Nazism in their movement stage, where there was considerable cross-fertilization (Reichardt 2009), a volume on the transnational origins of Italian Fascism (Alcalde 2016), and investigations of transnational currents in Eastern European fascism (Iordachi 2010) and throughout the whole of interwar Europe (Bauerkämper and Rossoliński-Liebe 2017). There have been reconstructions of the intense exchange of ideas and activists between Spanish and Italian fascist and neo-fascist subcultures for over six decades (Albanese and del Hierrero 2016) and the links between

French and Spanish fascisms (Mammone 2015), both of which eventually formed part of 'the global neo-fascist network'. A recent investigation of the links between Putin's Russia and the West European far right underlines just how many original subjects are being generated by neo-fascism's rapid evolution, despite being so marginalized (Shekhovtsov 2017).

Fascist studies seem ripe to enter a new phase of productivity. Whether it will be seen as building on the empathetic approach to the theory of fascism explored in this book, and thus represents a natural extension of it, or as a new departure that consigns talk of revolutionary nationalism and cultural palingenesis to the scholarly Hades of dead paradigms, will be for others to judge.

A new fascism?

Even if these tips about where 'cutting-edge' research in fascist studies is heading do not immediately prompt any epiphanies revealing a worthwhile research topic, as I suggested above, just studying an aspect of fascism in depth in a humanistic spirit has its own reward. It should help immunize you against fanaticism, against the demonizing of 'Others', against the adoption of a paranoid mindset about the enemies of the people who are allegedly destroying society and so must be removed or destroyed in their turn.

By the time this book is read, Western public opinion will probably still persist in seeing the threat of violence as coming almost exclusively from Islamist fanaticism, distracted from the permanent danger posed by the extreme right in all its forms to the health of democratic societies all over the world. Hopefully it will help act as a corrective to this bias. Given the continuing human need for leaders in times of crisis, and the adaptability and mutability of fascism itself, the advice which concentration camp survivor Primo Levi gave in 1986 in an interview to the US *New Republic* magazine still rings true today:

> Since it is difficult to distinguish true prophets from false, it is well to regard all prophets with suspicion. Yet it is clear that this formula is too simple to suffice in every case. A new

fascism, with its trail of intolerance, abuse, and servitude, can be born outside our country and imported into it, walking on tiptoe and calling itself by other names; or it can loose itself from within with such violence that it routs all defenses. At that point, wise counsel no longer serves, ... and one must find the strength to resist. But then, too, the memory of what happened in the heart of Europe, not very long ago, can serve as support and warning. (Levi 1986)

Levi's *If This is a Man* ([1947] 1960) is one of the greatest testimonies ever written to human physical, mental and moral survival in the face of systemic brutality and systematic dehumanization. To compose it with such lucidity and honesty, without hatred, bitterness or vindictiveness after spending eleven months in Auschwitz, he had to become an expert in understanding the nature of fascism, not through the mind of the historian or a political scientist, but through the tortured consciousness, organs, nerves and sinews of one of its millions of victims. Despite his immense physical and mental suffering, he somehow managed to retain not just his observational powers and reason, but his humanity. He lived to bear witness. The book's extraordinary power as a record of just one human being's experience of the attempted genocide of a whole race reminds us that, in the search to understand fascism as a 'key concept in political theory', we should never forget the often terrible human realities the term embraces. On the contrary, if we study fascism intelligently, we will find the historical and political imagination being sharpened and illuminated, not blunted and dimmed, and the humanism that should drive it deepened.

In the last analysis, what makes fascism a key concept is perhaps that, approached with methodological empathy and the humanistic zeal of the researcher, it should help us move from knowing *what* terrible things have happened and continue to happen in the midst of an advanced civilization in the name of the nation or race towards understanding at least partially *why*. In this way, both those who, despite all that has happened, are bent on making the fascist utopia a reality and those condemned to suffer as a result of their fanaticism can be brought closer to us than ever as human beings who form part of a proactive liberal militancy within modern democracies. And if a new form of right-wing threat to European values does tip-toe into our lives, or crash into our history like a meteorite, it might be useful to have a solid academic tradition of dealing with its antecedents to classify and evaluate it and so inject some empirically informed intelligence into society's response.

In a world awash with fake news, conspiracy theories and counterfactual fantasies, it is interesting to speculate what might have happened if such a body of *genuine* intelligence about Fascism and Nazism, based on an empathetic understanding of generic fascism which meant *taking its vision of the world seriously*, had existed in the mid-1930s. It might have enabled the Readers of the Western democracies to assess realistically the foreign policies of the Axis, and Hitler's long-term objectives for Europe, the East, and racial inferiors, principally but not only the Jews, and their realizability. Had the political and military masters of the Great Powers been prepared to accept its conclusions, and *acted on them*, there might have been no Second World War, and this book would have been very different – if it would have existed at all.

Notes

Chapter 1 Introduction

1   To explain why this is the case lies well beyond the remit of this book and falls into the province of specialists in the methodology and philosophy of the social sciences. These can draw on various epistemological pioneers to explain the impossibility of an 'objective' definition in the human sciences, such as the nineteenth-century sociologist Max Weber, the philosopher Heinrich Rickert, the psychological structuralist Lev Vygotsky or the co-founder of hermeneutics Paul Ricoeur (see Outhwaite 1983). The impossibility of an objective definition of all terms in the human sciences precludes the possibility of arriving at a total consensus or unanimity among experts about the meaning of any key concept and helps explain the tortuous definitional history of fascism to this day.

2   The 'ideal type' has much in common with the concepts *hypothetical construct* and *heuristic device*, and with equivalent terms found in any theory of knowledge or epistemology that stresses the active role of the mind or the conceptualizing faculty in abstracting from reality an idealized verbal model or paradigm of a generic phenomenon. The pioneer of sociology, Max Weber, first formulated the theory of the 'ideal type' as a conceptual device in the human sciences, formed through a conscious process of 'utopian abstraction' from empirical realities frequently referred to by the same generic term (he uses the example 'capitalism'). For a brief overview of the theory,

see William Outhwaite's article (2002: 280–2). This article also refers to Ludwig Wittgenstein's alternative but closely related theory of 'family resemblances' between the different phenomena referred to by the same generic term (he uses the example of the word 'game'). For a more detailed account of Weber's theory, see Burger (1976). However, it may interest those unfamiliar with the concept of an ideal type to read Max Weber's own description of it: 'an ideal type is formed by the one-sided accentuation [exaggeration: in German *Steigerung*] of one or more points of view' consistent with which 'concrete individual phenomena ... are arranged into a unified analytical construct [*Gedankenbild*, or 'thought-picture']. Such one-sided exaggeration – akin to the technique used in caricatures and cartoons to make a political point – is recognized by Weber as a heuristic fiction, or 'utopia [that] cannot be found empirically anywhere in reality' (Weber 1949: 90).

Chapter 2 Making Sense of Fascism

1 Some key works in English exploring these themes are: Manchester (1968); Turner (1985); Hayes (1987); Mason and Caplan (1995); Gregor (1998); Tooze (2007); Aly (2007).
2 For a major survey of postwar communist theories of fascism (in German), see Eichholz and Gossweiler (1980). Laclau (1977) and Woodley (2009) provide useful overviews in English.
3 For a sophisticated analysis of the electoral swing to Nazism even before 1933 as a 'normal' transclass phenomenon of disaffection with mainstream parties, see King et al. (2008).
4 For the ancient parable of the blind men and the elephant, see www.jainworld.com/literature/story25.htm.

Chapter 3 A Working Definition

1 For example, the theory of fascism expounded in *The Nature of Fascism* (1991) was based on my extensive study of a broad selection of primary sources carried out within the framework of doctoral research. These were selected as documents of the ideology of a wide range of putative fascist movements in a number of different languages, few of which were available in English. This process enabled both the pattern of themes

associated with 'palingenetic ultranationalism' to be established empirically in 'fascist' variants of the extreme right, and its absence to be considered a marker for a different genus of the extreme right. For an anthology of texts exemplifying the palingenetic myth in fascist nationalism based on this research, see Griffin (1995).

2   Though it has become the standard way of referring to the product of fascism's anthropological revolution, 'new man' in most fascist contexts refers to a new human being, female and male, and is thus a misleading term. In German, 'neuer Mensch' (usually translated as 'new man') is not gender-specific. For a corrective of gender bias in fascist studies, see Gottlieb (2000).

3   An allusion to Anderson (1983), a ground-breaking study of the role of shared fantasy in the construction of nationhood through imagining the national community.

Chapter 5 Neo-Fascism

1   The announcement that the WNCM had been founded prompted the online 'libertarian' journal *Counterpunch* to publish in September 2015 an excellent history of neo-fascism as an extraordinarily entangled international force. See Alexander Reid Ross, *A New Chapter in the Fascist Internationale*, www. counterpunch.org/2015/09/16/a-new-chapter-in-the-fascist-internationale/. For the list of the seventy-one groupuscules invited by the WNCM to attend (virtually?) the inaugural meeting in 2015, see www.sova-center.ru/files/xeno/parties.pdf.

2   E.g., in the US in 1999, the neo-Nazi skinhead Jessy Joe Roten fired shots into the home of a multi-racial family.

3   The murderer was the Ukrainian Pavlo Lapshyn, known for his racist and neo-Nazi activity in his home country.

4   A reference to the neo-Nazi Dylann Roof, who carried out the mass shooting at a Charleston church in 2015.

5   A reference to the murder by Thomas Mair in 2016 of the pro-EU United Kingdom Member of Parliament Jo Cox.

6   A reference to a gun attack carried out by the neo-Nazi James Wenneker von Brunn in 2009.

References and Bibliography

Abdel-Samad, Hamed (2016) *Islamic Fascism.* New York: Prometheus Books.

Adam, Peter (1992) *Art of the Third Reich.* New York: Harry N. Abrams.

Adamson, Walter (1980) *Hegemony and Revolution: A Study of Antonio Gramsci's Political and Cultural Theory.* Berkeley: University of California Press.

Adorno, Theodor W., Frenkel-Brunswik, Else, Levinson, Daniel J., and Sanford, R. Nevitt (1950) *The Authoritarian Personality.* New York: Harper & Row.

Affron, Mark, and Antliff, Mark (eds) (1998) *Fascist Visions: Art and Ideology in France and Italy.* Princeton, NJ: Princeton University Press.

Albanese, Matteo and del Hierrero, Pablo (2016) *Transnational Fascism in the Twentieth Century: Spain, Italy and the Global NeoFascist Network.* London: Bloomsbury.

Alcalde, Ángel (2016) 'War veterans and the transnational origins of Italian Fascism (1917–1919)', *Journal of Modern Italian Studies,* 21(4): 565–83.

Allardyce, Gilbert (1979) 'What fascism is not: Thoughts on the deflation of a concept', *American Historical Review,* 84(2): 367–98.

Aly, Götz (2007) *Hitler's Beneficiaries: Plunder, Racial War, and the Nazi Welfare State.* New York: Metropolitan Books.

Anderson, Benedict (1983) *Imagined Communities: Reflections on the Origin and Spread of Nationalism.* London: Verso.

Antliff, Mark (2007) *Avant-Garde Fascism: The Mobilization of*

Myth, Art and Culture in France, 1909–1939. Durham, NC: Duke University Press.

Arendt, Hannah (1951) *The Origins of Totalitarianism.* New York: Schocken.

Arnold, Edward (2000) *The Development of the Radical Right in France: From Boulanger to Le Pen.* London: Macmillan.

Arnstad, Henrik (2015) 'Ikea fascism: Metapedia and the internationalization of Swedish generic fascism', *Fascism,* 4(1): 103–17.

Baker, David (2006) 'The political economy of fascism: Myth *or* reality, or myth *and* reality?', *New Political Economy,* 11(2): 227–50.

Baldoli, Claudia (2003) *Exporting Fascism.* Oxford: Berg.

Bale, Jeffrey (2002) 'National revolutionary groupuscule and the resurgence of left-wing fascism: The case of France's Nouvelle Résistance', *Patterns of Prejudice,* 36(3): 24–49.

Ballent, Anna (2017) 'Faces of modernity in the architecture of the Peronist state, 1943–1955', *Fascism,* 6(1) [special issue: *Latin architecture in the era of fascism*].

Bardèche, Maurice (1961) *Qu'est-ce que le fascism?* Paris: Sept Couleurs.

Bartulin, Nevenko (2013) *The Racial Idea in the Independent State of Croatia: Origins and Theory.* Leiden: Brill.

Bauerkämper, Arnd and Rossoliński-Liebe, Grzegorz (2017) *Fascism without Borders: Transnational Connections and Cooperation between Movements and Regimes in Europe from 1918 to 1945.* Oxford: Berghahn Books.

Bauman, Zygmunt (1989) *Modernity and the Holocaust.* Ithaca, NY: Cornell University Press.

Bauman, Zygmunt (2000) *Liquid Modernity.* Cambridge: Polity.

Bauman, Zygmunt (2005) *Liquid Life.* Cambridge: Polity.

Beam, Louis (1992) 'Leaderless resistance', *The Seditionist,* no. 12, www.louisbeam.com/leaderless.htm.

Becker, Jasper (2002) 'China is a fascist country', *The Spectator,* 23 November 2002, www.prisonplanet.com/news_alert_112202_general2.html.

Beetham, David (1983) *Marxists in Face of Fascism.* Manchester: Manchester University Press.

Ben-Ghiat, Ruth (2001) *Fascist Modernities: Italy, 1922–1945.* Berkeley: University of California Press.

Beningfield, Jennifer (2006) *The Frightened Land: Land, Landscape and Politics in South Africa in the Twentieth Century.* London: Routledge.

Benjamin, Walter ([1936] 2008) *The Work of Art in the Age of Mechanical Reproduction.* London: Penguin.

Berezin, Mabel (1997) *Making the Fascist Self: The Political Culture of Interwar Italy*. Ithaca, NY: Cornell University Press.

Berggren, Lena (2002) 'Swedish fascism: why bother?', *Journal of Contemporary History*, 37(3): 395–417.

Berman, Marshall (1983) *All that is Solid Melts into Air: The Experience of Modernity*. New York: Verso.

Biver, Nico (2005) 'Trotskyist Parties', *Marxists Internet Archive*, www.broadleft.org/trotskyi.htm.

Blinkhorn, Martin (2000) *Fascism and the Right in Europe, 1919–1945*. Harlow: Longman.

Bloch, Ernst ([1935] 2009) *Heritage of our Times*. Cambridge: Polity.

Blomqvist, Anders, Iordachi, Constantin, and Trencsényi, Balázs (eds) (2013) *Hungary and Romania beyond National Narratives: Comparisons and Entanglements*. Bern: Peter Lang.

Borgese, Giuseppe (1934) 'The intellectual origins of Fascism', *Social Research*, 1(4): 458–85.

Bosworth, Richard (ed.) (2009) *The Oxford Handbook of Fascism*. Oxford: Oxford University Press.

Bottura, Juri (2009) *Spiritual Regeneration and Ultra-Nationalism: The Political Thought of Pedro Albizu Campos and Plínio Salgado in 1930s Puerto Rico and Brazil*. Nashville: Vanderbilt University.

Bracher, Karl (1973) *The German Dictatorship: The Origins, Structure, and Consequences of National Socialism*. London: Penguin.

Braun, Emily (2000) *Mario Sironi and Italian Modernism: Art and Politics under Fascism*. Cambridge: Cambridge University Press.

Brooker, Paul (1991) *The Faces of Fraternalism: Nazi Germany, Fascist Italy, and Imperial Japan*. Oxford: Oxford University Press.

Buc, Philippe (2015) *Holy War, Martyrdom, and Terror: Christianity, Violence, and the West*. Philadelphia: University of Pennsylvania Press.

Bucur, Maria (2002) *Eugenics and Modernization in Interwar Romania*. Pittsburgh: University of Pittsburgh Press.

Bullock, Alan (ed.) (1977) *Fontana Dictionary of Political Thought*. London: Fontana.

Burger, Thomas (1976) *Max Weber's Theory of Concept Formation: History, Laws and Ideal Types*. Durham, NC: Duke University Press.

Burleigh, Michael, and Wippermann, Wolfgang (1991) *The Racial State: Germany 1933–1945*. Cambridge: Cambridge University Press.

Caplan, Jane (1977) 'Theories of fascism: Nicos Poulantzas as historian', *History Workshop Journal*, 3(1): 83–100.

Caplan, Jane (ed.) (1995) *Nazism, Fascism and the Working Class: Essays by Tim Mason*. Cambridge: Cambridge University Press.

Carsten, Francis (1967) *The Rise of Fascism*. London: Methuen.

Cassata, Francesco (2008) *'La difesa della razza': politica, ideologia e immagine del razzismo fascista*. Turin: Einaudi.

Cassata, Francesco (2011) *Building the New Man: Eugenics, Racial Science and Genetics in Twentieth-Century Italy*. Budapest: Central European University Press.

Castelli Gattinara, Pietro and Froio, Caterina (2014) 'Discourse and practice of violence in the Italian extreme right: frames, symbols, and identity-building in CasaPound Italia', *International Journal of Conflict and Violence*, 8(1): 155–70.

Cerasi, Laura (2017) 'Rethinking Italian corporatism: Crossing borders between corporatist projects in the late liberal era and the Fascist corporatist state', in António Costa Pinto (ed.), *Corporatism and Fascism: The Corporatist Wave in Europe*. London: Routledge, pp. 103–23.

Cheles, Luciano (1991) '"Nostalgia dell'avvenire": The propaganda of the Italian far right between tradition and innovation', in Cheles, Ronnie Ferguson and Michalina Vaughan (eds), *Neofascism in Europe*. London: Longman.

Cinpoes, Radu (2016) *Nationalism and Identity in Romania: A History of Extreme Politics from the Birth of the State to EU Accession*. London: I. B. Tauris.

Clark, Roland (2012) *European Fascists and Local Activists: Romania's Legion of the Archangel Michael*. Dissertation, University of Pittsburgh, http://d-scholarship.pitt.edu/11837/.

Cobo Romero, Francisco, Hernández Burgos, Claudio, and del Arco Blanco, Miguel Ángel (eds) (2016) *Fascismo y modernismo: política y cultura en la Europa de entreguerras (1918–1945)*. Granada: Comares.

Coogan, Kevin (1999) *Dreamer of the Day: Francis Parker Yockey and the Postwar Fascist International*. New York: Autonomedia.

Copsey, Nigel (1996) *Contemporary British Fascism: The British Fascist Party and the Quest for Legitimacy*. Basingstoke: Palgrave Macmillan.

Copsey, Nigel (2007) 'Changing course or changing clothes? Reflections on the ideological evolution of the British National Party 1999–2006', *Patterns of Prejudice*, 41(1): 61–82.

Costa Pinto, António (2000) *The Blue Shirts: Portuguese Fascists and the New State*. Boulder, CO: Social Science Monographs.

Costa Pinto, António (2017) *Corporatism and Fascism: The Corporatist Wave in Europe*. London: Routledge.

Costa Pinto, António and Kallis, Aristotle (eds) (2014) *Rethinking Fascism and Dictatorship in Europe*. Basingstoke: Palgrave Macmillan.

Cronin, Mike (1996) *The Failure of British Fascism: The Far Right and the Fight for Political Recognition*. London: Macmillan.

Cullingford, Elizabeth (1981) *Yeats, Ireland and Fascism*. London: Macmillan.

Dagnino, Jorge (2016) 'The myth of the New Man in Italian Fascist ideology', *Fascism*, 5(2): 130–48.

Dahrendorf, Ralf (1968) *Society and Democracy in Germany*. London: Weidenfeld & Nicolson.

de Benoist, Alain (1977) *Vu de droite: anthologie critique des idées contemporaines*. Paris: Copernic.

de Benoist, Alain and Champetier, Charles (2012) *Manifesto for a European Renaissance*. London: Arktos.

De Felice, Renzo (1976) *Fascism: An Informal Introduction to its Theory and Practice*. New Brunswick, NJ: Transaction Books.

De Felice, Renzo (1977) *Interpretations of Fascism*. Cambridge, MA: Harvard University Press.

De Grand, Alexander (1991) 'Cracks in the façade: the failure of Fascist totalitarianism in Italy 1935–9', *European History Quarterly*, 21(4): 515–35.

De Grand, Alexander (1996) *Fascist Italy and Nazi Germany: The 'Fascist' Style of Rule*. New York: Routledge.

De Grazia, Victoria (1992) *Women under Fascism*. Berkeley: University of California Press.

Deák, István (1983) 'What was fascism?', *New York Review of Books*, 3 March.

Deakin, William (1962) *The Brutal Friendship: Mussolini, Hitler and the Fall of Italian Fascism*. New York: Harper & Row.

Degrelle, Léon (1969) *Hitler pour mille ans*. Paris: Table Ronde.

Deutsch, Sandra (2013) 'Anti-Semitism and the Chilean Movimiento Nacional Socialista, 1932–41', in Simo Muir and Hana Worthen (eds), *Finland's Holocaust: Silences of History*. Basingstoke: Palgrave Macmillan.

Dimitrov, Georgi (1935) 'The class character of Fascism', in *The Fascist Offensive and the Tasks of the Communist International in the Struggle of the Working Class against Fascism* (main report delivered at the Seventh World Congress of the Communist International), www.marxists.org/reference/archive/dimitrov/works/1935/ 08_02.htm.

Dobkowski, Michael and Wallimann, Isidor (eds) (1989) *Radical*

Perspectives on the Rise of Fascism in Germany, 1919 to 1945. New York: Monthly Review Press.

Dobratz, Betty (1997) *White Power, White Pride! The White Separatist Movement in the United States.* London: Twayne.

Drucker, Peter F. (1939) *The End of Economic Man: A Study of the New Totalitarianism.* London: Heinemann.

Duggan, Christopher (2012) *Fascist Voices: An Intimate History of Mussolini's Italy.* London: Bodley Head.

Dyckhoff, Tom (2002) 'Mies and the Nazis', *Guardian*, 30 November, www.theguardian.com/artanddesign/2002/nov/30/architecture.artsfeatures.

Eatwell, Roger (1992) 'Towards a new model of generic fascism', *Journal of Theoretical Politics*, 2(2): 161–94.

Eatwell, Roger (1995) *Fascism: A History.* London: Chatto & Windus.

Eatwell, Roger (2006) 'Explaining fascism and ethnic cleansing: The three dimensions of charisma and the four dark sides of nationalism', *Political Science Review*, 4(3): 263–78.

Eatwell, Roger (2009) 'The nature of "generic fascism": The "fascist minimum" and the "fascist matrix"', in Constantin Iordachi (ed.), *Comparative Fascist Studies: New Perspectives.* Abingdon: Routledge.

Eco, Umberto (1995) 'Eternal fascism: Fourteen ways of looking at a blackshirt', *New York Review of Books*, 22 June, pp. 12–15.

Eichholz, Dietrich and Gossweiler, Kurt (eds) (1980) *Faschismus-Forschung: Positionen, Probleme, Polemik.* East Berlin: Akademie Verlag.

Eisenberg, Dennis (1967) *The Re-emergence of Fascism.* London: MacGibbon & Kee.

Emberland, Terje (2015) 'Neither Hitler nor Quisling: the Ragnarok circle and oppositional National Socialism in Norway', *Fascism*, 4(2): 119–33.

Esposito, Fernando (ed.) (2015a) *Journal of Modern European History*, 13(1) [special issue: *Fascist Temporalities*].

Esposito, Fernando (2015b) *Fascism, Aviation and Mythical Modernity.* Basingstoke: Palgrave Macmillan.

Evans, Richard (2002) *Telling Lies about Hitler: The Holocaust, History and the David Irving Trial.* London: Verso.

Evans, Richard (2004) *The Coming of the Third Reich: How the Nazis Destroyed Democracy and Seized Power in Germany.* New York: Penguin.

Evans, Richard (2009) *The Third Reich at War, 1939–1945.* London: Penguin.

Evola, Julius ([1953] 2002) *Men among the Ruins: Post-War*

Reflections of a Radical Traditionalist. Rochester, VT: Inner Traditions.

Evola, Julius ([1961] 2003) *Ride the Tiger: A Survival Manual for the Aristocrats of the Soul.* Rochester, VT: Inner Traditions.

Feldman, Matthew (2013) *Ezra Pound's Fascist Propaganda, 1935–1945.* Basingstoke: Palgrave Macmillan.

Feldman, Matthew and Jackson, Paul (eds) (2014) *Doublespeak. The Rhetoric of the Far Right since 1945.* Stuttgart: Ibidem.

Feldman, Matthew, Dagnino, Jorge and Stocker, Paul (eds) (2017) *The 'New Man' in Radical Right Ideology and Practice, 1919–45.* London: Bloomsbury.

Fernández Prieto, Lourenzo, Pan-Montojo, Juan and Cabo, Miguel (eds) (2014) *Agriculture in the Age of Fascism: Authoritarian Technocracy* and *Rural Modernization, 1922–1945.* Turnhout: Brepols.

Ferraresi, Franco (1996) *Threats to Democracy: The Radical Right in Italy after the War.* Princeton, NJ: Princeton University Press.

Forgacs, David (1994) 'Fascism, violence and modernity', in Jana Howlett and Rod Mengham (eds), *The Violent Muse: Violence and the Artistic Imagination in Europe, 1910–1939.* Manchester: Manchester University Press, pp. 5–21.

Fourth Congress of the Comintern (1922) *Theses on Communist Tactics*, 5 December, www.marxists.org/history/international/comintern/4th-congress/tactics.htm.

Freeden, Michael (1994) 'Political concepts and ideological morphology', *Journal of Political Philosophy*, 2(2): 140–64.

Freeden, Michael (1996) *Ideologies and Political Theory.* Oxford: Clarendon Press.

Fritzsche, Peter (1996) 'Nazi modern', *Modernism/Modernity*, 3(1): 1–22.

Fritzsche, Peter and Hellbeck, Jochen (2009) 'The New Man in Stalinist Russia and Nazi Germany', in Michael Geyer and Sheila Fitzpatrick (eds), *Beyond Totalitarianism: Stalinism and Nazism Compared.* Cambridge: Cambridge University Press, pp. 302–44.

Fromm, Erich (1941) *Escape from Freedom.* New York: Farrar & Reinhart; pubd in the UK as *The Fear of Freedom*, London: Routledge & Kegan Paul.

Furlong, Paul (2011) *Social and Political Thought of Julius Evola.* Abingdon: Routledge.

Gable, Gerry and Jackson, Paul (2011) *Lone Wolves: Myth or Reality?* Ilford: Searchlight.

Gellately, Robert (1991) 'Rethinking the Nazi terror system: a historiographical analysis', *German Studies Review*, 14(1): 23–38.

Gentile, Emilio (1972) *'La Voce' e l'età giolittiana.* Milan: Pan.

Gentile, Emilio (1975) *Le origini dell'ideologia fascista (1918–1925)*. Bari: Laterza.

Gentile, Emilio (1976) *Mussolini e La Voce*. Florence: Sansoni.

Gentile, Emilio (1982) *Il mito dello stato nuovo: dall'antigiolittismo al fascismo*. Rome: Laterza.

Gentile, Emilio (1990) 'Fascism as political religion', *Journal of Contemporary History*, 25(2/3): 229–51.

Gentile, Emilio (1996) *The Sacralization of Politics in Fascist Italy*. Cambridge, MA: Harvard University Press.

Gentile, Emilio (1997) 'The myth of national regeneration in Italy: From modernist avant-garde to Fascism', in Matthew Affron and Mark Antliff (eds), *Fascist Visions*. Princeton, NJ: Princeton University Press, pp. 25–45.

Gentile, Emilio (2003) *The Struggle for Modernity: Nationalism, Futurism, and Fascism*. Westport, CT: Praeger.

Gentile, Emilio (2004) 'Fascism, totalitarianism and political religion: Definitions and critical reflections on criticism of an interpretation', *Totalitarian Movements and Political Religion*, 5(3): 326–75.

Gentile, Emilio (2005) 'The Fascist anthropological revolution', in Guido Bonsaver and Robert Gordon (eds), *Culture, Censorship and the State in Twentieth-Century Italy*. Oxford: Legenda, pp. 22–33.

Gentile, Emilio (2006) *Politics as Religion*. Princeton, NJ: Princeton University Press.

Georgescu, Tudor (2010) 'Ethnic minorities and the eugenic promise: The Transylvanian Saxon experiment with national renewal in interwar Romania', *European Review of History/Revue européenne d'histoire*, 17(6): 861–80.

Germinario, Francesco (2009) *Fascismo e antisemitismo: progetto razziale e ideologia totalitarian*. Rome: Laterza.

GIRDS (German Institute on Radicalization and De-Radicalization Studies) (2017) 'Database on terrorism in Germany: Right-wing extremism and jihadism', www.girds.org/projects/database-on-terrorism-in-germany-right-wing-extremism.

Goldberg, Jonah (2008) *Liberal Fascism*. New York: Doubleday.

Goldhagen, Daniel (2007) *Hitler's Willing Executioners: Ordinary Germans and the Holocaust*. New York: Knopf Doubleday.

Goodhart, David (2017) *The Road to Somewhere: The Populist Revolt and the Future of Politics*. London: Hurst.

Goodrick-Clarke, Nicholas (2003) *Black Sun: Aryan Cults, Esoteric Nazism and the Politics of Identity*. New York: New York University Press.

Goodrick-Clarke, Nicholas (2004) *The Occult Roots of Nazism:*

Secret Aryan Cults and their Influence on Nazi Ideology. London: I. B. Tauris.

Goslan, Richard (ed.) (1998) *Fascism's Return: Scandal, Revision, and Ideology since 1980*. Lincoln: University of Nebraska Press.

Gottlieb, Julie (2000) *Feminine Fascism: Women in Britain's Fascist Movement, 1923–1945*. London: I.B. Tauris.

Gottlieb, Julie and Linehan, Thomas (eds) (2004) *The Culture of Fascism: Visions of the Far Right in Britain*. London: I.B. Tauris.

Gregor, A. James (1974) *Interpretations of Fascism*. New York: Transaction Books.

Gregor, A. James (1979) *Italian Fascism and Development*. Princeton, NJ: Princeton University Press.

Gregor, A. James (1999) *Phoenix: Fascism in our Time*. New Brunswick, NJ: Transaction Books.

Gregor, A. James (2006) *The Search for Neofascism: The Use and Abuse of Social Science*. New York: Cambridge University Press.

Gregor, Neil (1998) *Daimler-Benz in the Third Reich*. New Haven, CT: Yale University Press.

Griech-Polelle, Beth Ann (2015) 'The Catholic episcopacy and the National Socialist state', in Jan Nelis, Anne Morelli and Danny Praet (eds), *Catholicism and Fascism in Europe 1918–1945*. Hildesheim: Georg Olms.

Griffin, Roger (1991) *The Nature of Fascism*. London: Pinter.

Griffin, Roger (1994) Integration and identification: Conflicting aspects of the human need for self-transcendence within ideological communities', *History of European Ideas*, 18(1): 11–23.

Griffin, Roger (1995) *Fascism*. Oxford: Oxford University Press.

Griffin, Roger (1996) 'British fascism: The ugly duckling', in Mike Cronin (ed.), *The Failure of British Fascism: The Far Right and the Fight for Political Recognition*. London: Macmillan.

Griffin, Roger (1998) *International Fascism: Theories, Causes and the New Consensus*. London: Arnold.

Griffin, Roger (1999) 'Net gains and GUD reactions: Patterns of prejudice in a neo-fascist groupuscule', *Patterns of Prejudice*, 33(2): 31–50.

Griffin, Roger (2000a) 'Interregnum or endgame? The radical right in the "post-fascist" era', *Journal of Political Ideologies*, 5(2): 163–78.

Griffin, Roger (2000b) 'Between metapolitics and apoliteia: The Nouvelle Droite's strategy for conserving the fascist vision in the "interregnum"', *Modern & Contemporary France*, 8(1): 35–53.

Griffin, Roger (2002) 'The primacy of culture: The current growth (or manufacture) of consensus within fascist studies', *Journal of Contemporary History*, 37(1): 21–43.

Griffin, Roger (2003a) '"Racism" or "rebirth"? The case for granting German citizenship to the alien concept "generic fascism"', in Werner Loh and Wolfgang Wippermann (eds), *Faschismus kontrovers*. Stuttgart: Lucius & Lucius, pp. 81–9.

Griffin, Roger (2003b) 'From slime mould to rhizome: An introduction to the groupuscular right', *Patterns of Prejudice*, 37(1): 27–50.

Griffin, Roger (2004) 'Withstanding the rush of time: The prescience of G. L. Mosse's anthropological approach to fascism' in Stanley Payne, David Sorkin and John Tortorice (eds), *What History Tells: George L. Mosse and the Culture of Modern Europe*. Madison: University of Wisconsin Press.

Griffin, Roger (2005) 'Cloister or cluster? The implications of Emilio Gentile's ecumenical theory of political religion for the study of extremism', *Totalitarian Movements and Political Religions*, 6(1): 33–52.

Griffin, Roger (2007) *Modernism and Fascism: The Sense of a Beginning under Mussolini and Hitler*. Basingstoke: Palgrave Macmillan.

Griffin, Roger (2008) 'Europe for the Europeans: Fascist myths of the European New Order, 1922–1992', in Matthew Feldman (ed.), *A Fascist Century: Essays by Roger Griffin*. London: Palgrave: 132–80.

Griffin, Roger (2012a) 'Studying Fascism in a Postfascist Age: From New Consensus to New Wave?', *Fascism*, 1(1): 1–17.

Griffin, Roger (2012b) *Terrorist's Creed: Fanatical Violence and the Human Search for Meaning*. London: Palgrave Macmillan.

Griffin, Roger (2015a) 'Decentering comparative fascist studies', *Fascism*, 4(2): 103–18.

Griffin, Roger (2015b) 'Fixing solutions: Fascist temporalities as remedies for liquid modernity', *Journal of Modern European History*, 13(1): 5–23.

Griffin, Roger (2017) 'Futures set in stone: architectural projections of a "New Order" under interwar dictatorships', *Fascism*, 6(2) [special issue: *Latin Architecture in the Era of Fascism*].

Griffin, Roger, Umland, Andreas, and Loh, Werner (2014) Fascism *Past and Present, West and East: An International Debate on Concepts and Cases in the Comparative Study of the Extreme Right*. Stuttgart: Ibidem.

Haglund, Åke (1975) 'Maoism: A new religious formation in the People's Republic of China', Scripta Instituti *Donneriani Aboensis*, 7: 43–54.

Hagtvet, Bernt and Kühnl, Reinhart (1980) 'Contemporary approaches to fascism: A survey of paradigms', in Stein Larsen, Bernt Hagtvet and Jan Petter Myklebust (eds), *Who Were the Fascists? Social Roots of European Fascism.* Oslo: Universitetsforlaget, pp. 26–51.

Hamilton, Alistair (1971) *The Appeal of Fascism: A Study of Intellectuals and Fascism, 1919–45.* New York: Blond.

Hayes, Peter (1987) *Industry and Ideology: IG Farben in the Nazi Era.* Cambridge: Cambridge University Press.

Herf, Jeffrey (1984) *Reactionary Modernism: Technology, Culture and Politics in Weimar and the Third Reich.* Cambridge: Cambridge University Press.

Herzstein, Robert (1982) *When Nazi Dreams Come True: The Third Reich's Internal Struggle over the Future of Europe after a German Victory: A Look at the Nazi Mentality 1939–45.* London: Abacus.

Hitler, Adolf (1942) 'Speech of 6 September 1938', in Norman H. Baynes (ed.), *The Speeches of Adolf Hitler, April 1922–August 1939.* Oxford: Oxford University Press.

Hitler, Adolf ([1926] 1992) *Mein Kampf*, Vol. 2. London: Pimlico.

Horn, David (1994) *Social Bodies: Science, Reproduction, and Italian Modernity.* Princeton, NJ: Princeton University Press.

Horowitz, Jason (2017) 'Steve Bannon cited Italian thinker who inspired Fascists', *New York Times*, 10 February, www.nytimes.com/2017/02/10/world/europe/bannon-vatican-julius-evola-fascism.html.

Huggler, Justin (2015) 'Germany's Pegida anti-Islam movement vows to continue protests in Berlin and Munich', *Telegraph*, 19 January, www.telegraph.co.uk/news/worldnews/europe/germany/11355318/Germanys-Pegida-anti-Islam-movement-vows-to-continue-protests-in-Berlin-and-Munich.html.

Iordachi, Constantin (ed.) (2009) *Comparative Fascist Studies: New Perspectives.* Abingdon: Routledge.

Iordachi, Constantin (2010) 'Fascism in interwar East Central and Southeastern Europe: Toward a new transnational research agenda', *East-Central Europe*, 37(2–3): 161–213.

Ira, Kumaran (2016) 'Neo-fascist Marine Le Pen launches 2017 French presidential election bid', 22 September, www.wsws.org/en/articles/2016/09/22/fnat-s22.html.

Jackson, Paul (2017) *Colin Jordan and Britain's Neo-Nazi Movement: Hitler's Echo.* London: Bloomsbury.

Jünger, Ernst (1922) *Der Kampf als inneres Erlebnis.* Berlin: E. S. Mittler.

Jünger, Ernst (1932) *Der Arbeiter: Herrschaft und Gestalt.* Hamburg: Hanseatische Verlagsanstalt.

Kallis, Aristotle (2000) *Fascist Ideology: Territory and Expansionism in Italy and Germany, 1922–1945.* London: Routledge.

Kallis, Aristotle (ed.) (2003) *The Fascism Reader.* London, Routledge.

Kallis, Aristotle (2008) *Genocide and Fascism: The Eliminationist Drive in Fascist Europe.* London: Routledge.

Kallis, Aristotle (2010) 'Neither fascist nor authoritarian: The 4th of August regime in Greece (1936–1941) and the dynamics of fascistisation in 1930s Europe', *East Central Europe*, 37(2–3): 303–30.

Kallis, Aristotle (2014) *The Third Rome, 1922–1943: The Making of the Fascist Capital.* Basingstoke: Palgrave McMillian.

Kallis, Aristotle (2016) 'From CAUR to EUR: Italian Fascism, the "myth of Rome" and the pursuit of international primacy', *Patterns of Prejudice*, 50(4–5): 359–77.

Kaplan, Jeffrey (1997) *Radical Religion in America: Millenarian Movements from the Far Right to the Children of Noah.* Syracuse, NY: Syracuse University Press.

Kaplan, Jeffrey and Lööw, Heléne (2002) *The Cultic Milieu: Oppositional Subcultures in an Age of Globalization.* Walnut Creek, CA: AltaMira Press.

Karvonen, Lauri (1988) *From White to Blue-and-Black: Finnish Fascism, in the Inter-War Era.* Helsinki: Finnish Society of Sciences.

Kasekamp, Andreas (2000) *The Radical Right in Interwar Estonia.* London: Palgrave Macmillan.

Kellner, Douglas (1989) *Critical Theory, Marxism, and Modernity.* Baltimore: Johns Hopkins University Press.

Kennedy, Paul (1987) *The Rise and Fall of Great Powers: Economic Change and Military Conflict from 1500 to 2000.* New York: Random House.

Kershaw, Ian (1989) 'The Nazi state: an exceptional state?', *New Left Review*, 1(176): 47–67.

Kershaw, Ian (1998) *Hitler: 1889–1936: Hubris.* Harmondsworth: Penguin.

Kershaw, Ian (1999) *Hitler: 1936–1945: Nemesis.* Harmondsworth: Penguin.

Kershaw, Ian ([1985] 2000) *The Nazi Dictatorship.* London: Arnold.

Kershaw, Ian (2004) 'Hitler and the uniqueness of Nazism', *Journal of Contemporary History*, 39(2): 239–54.

Kershaw, Ian (2015) 'Out of the ashes: Europe's rebirth after the Second World War, 1945–1949', *Journal of the British Academy*, 3: 167–83.

King, Gary, Rosen, Ori, Tanner, Martin and Wagner, Alexander (2008) 'Ordinary economic voting behavior in the extraordinary election of Adolf Hitler', *Journal of Economic History*, 68: 951–96.

Kitchen, Martin (1973) 'August Thalheimer's theory of fascism', *Journal of the History of Ideas*, 34(1): 67–78.

Klemperer, Victor (2006) *Lingua Tertii Imperii: A Philologist's Notebook*. London: Continuum.

Koehler, Daniel (2014) 'The German "National Socialist Underground" (NSU)', in Paul Jackson and Anton Shekhovtsov (eds), *The Post-War Anglo-American Far Right: A Special Relationship of Hate*. Basingstoke: Palgrave Macmillan.

Koehler, Daniel (2016) *Right-Wing Terrorism in the 21st Century: The 'National Socialist Underground' and the History of Terror from the Far Right in Germany*. London: Routledge.

Koenigsberg, Richard (2015) 'The nation as an immortal organism', www.libraryofsocialscience.com/newsletter/posts/2015/2015-02-05-RAK-organism.html.

Koonz, Claudia (2005) *The Nazi Conscience*. Cambridge, MA: Harvard University Press.

Kornhauser, William (1959) *The Politics of Mass Society*. Glencoe, IL: Free Press.

Koselleck, Reinhart (2002) 'The temporalization of Utopia', in *The Practice of Conceptual History: Timing History, Spacing Concepts*. Stanford, CA: Stanford University Press, pp. 84–99.

Kroll, Frank-Lothar (1999) *Utopie als Ideologie: Geschichtsdenken und politisches Handeln im Dritten Reich*. Paderborn: Ferdinand Schöningh.

Laclau, Ernesto (1977) 'Fascism and ideology', in Laclau, *Politics and Ideology in Marxist Theory: Capitalism, Fascism, Populism*. London: NLB, pp. 81–142.

Laing, Ronald (1960) *The Divided Self: An Existential Study in Sanity and Madness*. Harmondsworth: Penguin.

Laqueur, Walter (ed.) (1976) *Fascism: A Reader's Guide: Analyses, Interpretations, Bibliography*. Berkeley: University of California Press.

Larsen, Stein (ed.) (2001) *Fascism Outside Europe: The European Impulse against Domestic Conditions in the Diffusion of Global Fascism*. New York: Columbia University Press.

Larsen, Stein, Hagtvet, Bernt, and Myklebust, Jan Petter (eds) (1980) *Who Were the Fascists? Social Roots of European Fascism*. Oslo: Universitetsforlaget.

Lasswell, Harold (1933) 'The psychology of Hitlerism', *Political Quarterly*, 4(3): 373–84.

Law, Randall (2016) *Terrorism: A History*. London: Wiley.

Lebor, Adam (1997) *Hitler's Secret Bankers: The Myth of Swiss Neutrality during the Holocaust*. New York: Citadel Press.

Ledeen, Michael (1972) *Universal Fascism: The Theory and Practice of the Fascist International, 1928–1936*. New York: Howard Fertig.

Lee, Martin (1999) *The Beast Reawakens: Fascism's Resurgence from Hitler's Spymasters to Today's Neo-Nazi Groups and Right-Wing Extremists*. London: Routledge.

Lentin, Alana (2000) '"Race", racism and anti-racism: Challenging contemporary classifications', *Social Identities Journal for the Study of Race, Nation and Culture*, 6(1): 91–106.

Levi, Primo ([1947] 1960) *If This is a Man*, trans. Stuart Woolf. London: Deutsch.

Levi, Primo (1986) 'Primo Levi's heartbreaking, heroic answers to the most common questions he was asked about "Survival in Auschwitz"', *New Republic*, 17 February, https://newrepublic.com/article/119959/interview-primo-levi-survival-auschwitz.

Levine, Gene, and Priester, Gary (2008) *Hidden Treasures: 3-D Stereograms*. New York: Sterling.

Levy, Jack (2012) 'Too important to leave to the other: History and political science in the study of international relations', *International Security*, 22(1): 22–33.

Lewis, Paul (2002) *Latin Fascist Elites: The Mussolini, Franco, and Salazar Regimes*. Westport, CT: Greenwood Press.

Lifton, Robert (1993) *The Protean Self: Human Resilience in an Age of Fragmentation*. New York: HarperCollins.

Linehan, Thomas (2007) 'On the side of Christ: Fascist clerics in 1930s Britain', *Totalitarian Movements and Political Religions*, 8(2): 287–301 [special issue: '*Clerical Fascism*' in *Interwar Europe*].

Linton, Derek (1989) 'Bonapartism, Fascism, and the Collapse of the Weimar Republic', in Michael N. Dobkowski and Isidor Wallimann (eds), *Radical Perspectives on the Rise of Fascism in Germany, 1919–1945*. New York: Monthly Review Press, pp. 100–27.

Linz, Juan (1976) 'Some notes toward a comparative study of fascism in sociological historical perspective', in Walter Laqueur (ed.), *Fascism: A Reader's Guide*. Berkeley: University of California Press, pp. 3–121.

Linz, Juan (1980) 'Political space and fascism as a late-comer', in Stein Larsen, Bernt Hagtvet and Jan Petter Myklebust (eds),

Who Were the Fascists? Social Roots of European Fascism. Oslo: Universitetsforlag, pp. 153–89.

Lipset, Seymour Martin (1960) *Political Man: The Social Bases of Politics*. Garden City, NY: Doubleday.

Lipstadt, Deborah (1993) *Denying the Holocaust: The Growing Assault on Truth and Memory*. New York: Free Press.

Lowles, Nick, and Silver, Steve (1998) *White Noise: Inside the International Nazi Skinhead Scene*. London: Searchlight.

Lukács, György ([1952] 1980) *The Destruction of Reason*. London: Merlin Press.

Lunn, Eugene (1985) *Marxism and Modernism: An Historical Study of Lukács, Brecht, Benjamin, and Adorno*. New York: Verso.

Lyons, Matthew N. ([1997] 2016) 'What is fascism?', www.politicalresearch.org/2016/12/12/what-is-fascism-2/#sthash.RziH5ojF.dpbs.

Macklin, Graham (2007) *Very Deeply Dyed in Black: Sir Oswald Mosley and the Resurrection of British Fascism after 1945*. London: I. B. Tauris.

McLagen, Graeme and Lowles, Nick (2000) *Mr Evil: The Secret Life of Racist Pub Bomber and Killer David Copeland*. London: Abe Books.

Maertz, George (2017) 'Eugenic art: Hitler's utopian aesthetic', in Matthew Feldman, Jorge Dagnino and Paul Stocker (eds), *The 'New Man' in Radical Right Ideology and Practice, 1919–45*. London: Bloomsbury.

Mammone, Andrea (2015) *Transnational Neofascism in France and Italy*. Cambridge: Cambridge University Press.

Manchester, William (1968) *The Arms of Krupp*. Boston: Little, Brown.

Mangan, J. A. (ed.) (2000) *Superman Supreme: Fascist Body as Political Icon – Global Fascism*. London: Routledge.

Mann, Michael (2004) *Fascists*. Cambridge: Cambridge University Press.

Markwick, Roger (2009) 'Communism: fascism's "other"', in Richard Bosworth (ed.) *The Oxford Handbook of Fascism*. Oxford: Oxford University Press, pp. 339–61.

Marvin, Carolyn and Ingle, David (1999) *Blood Sacrifice and the Nation: Totem Rituals and the American Flag*. Cambridge: Cambridge University Press.

Marx, Christoph (2009) *Oxwagon Sentinel: Radical Afrikaner Nationalism and the History of the 'Ossewabrandwag'*. Berlin: Lit.

Marxists Internet Archive Encyclopedia (1999–2008) 'Fascism', www.marxists.org/glossary/terms/f/a.htm#fascism.

Mason, Timothy ([1966] 1972) 'The primacy of politics – politics and economics in National Socialist Germany', in Henry A. Turner (ed.), *Nazism and the Third Reich*. New York: Quadrangle Books, pp. 175–200.

Maulsby, Lucy (2014) *Fascism, Architecture, and the Claiming of Modern Milan, 1922–1943*. Toronto: University of Toronto Press.

Metapedia (2017) 'Fascism (broad sense)', http://en.metapedia.org/wiki/Fascism_(broad_sense).

Michael, George (2006) *The Enemy of my Enemy: The Alarming Convergence of Militant Islam and the Extreme Right*. Lawrence: University Press of Kansas.

Michaud, Eric (2004) *The Cult of Art in Nazi Germany*. Stanford, CA: Stanford University Press.

Michel, Lou and Herbeck, Dan (2001) *American Terrorist: Timothy McVeigh & The Oklahoma City Bombing*. New York: HarperCollins.

Moffitt, Benjamin (2016) *The Global Rise of Populism: Performance, Political Style, and Representation*. Stanford, CA: Stanford University Press.

Mohler, Armin (1950) *Die Konservative Revolution in Deutschland 1918–1932*. Stuttgart: Friedrich Vorwerk.

Moore, Barrington (1966) *Social Origins of Dictatorship and Democracy: Lord and Peasant in the Making of the Modern World*. Boston: Beacon Press.

Morgan, Philip (2003) *Fascism in Europe 1919–1945*. London: Routledge.

Mosley, Oswald (1968) *My Life*. London: Nelson.

Mosse, George L. (1964) *The Crisis of German Ideology: Intellectual Origins of the Third Reich*. New York: Grosset & Dunlap.

Mosse, George L. (1966a) 'The genesis of fascism', *Journal of Contemporary History*, 1(1): 14–26 [special issue on international fascism].

Mosse, George L. (ed.) (1966b) *Nazi Culture: Intellectual, Cultural and Social Life in the Third Reich*. Wisconsin: University of Wisconsin Press.

Mosse, George L. (1974) *The Nationalization of the Masses: Political Symbolism and Mass Movements in Germany from the Napoleonic Wars through the Third Reich*. New York: Howard Fertig.

Mosse, George L. (ed.) (1979) *International Fascism: New Thoughts and New Approaches*. London: Sage.

Mosse, George L. (1990) *Fallen Soldiers: Reshaping the Memory of the World Wars*. New York: Oxford University Press.

Mosse, George L. (1999) *The Fascist Revolution: Toward a General Theory of Fascism*. New York: Howard Fertig.

Mosse, George L. (2000) *Confronting History: A Memoir*. Madison: University of Wisconsin Press.

Moța, Ion (1933) 'Sub povara remanențelor', *Axa*, 2(23): 3.

Mozaffari, Mehdi (2017) *Islamism: A New Totalitarianism*. London: Lynne Rienner.

Mudde, Cas (2007) *Populist Radical Right Parties in Europe*. Cambridge: Cambridge University Press.

Mudde, Cas and Kaltwasser, Cristóbal (2017) *Populism: A Very Short Introduction*. Oxford: Oxford University Press.

Mühlberger, Detlef (1991) *Hitler's Followers: Studies in the Sociology of the Nazi Movement*. London: Routledge.

Mühlberger, Detlef (ed.) (1998) *The Social Basis of European Fascist Movements*. London: Croom Helm.

Mulsoff, Andreas (2010) *Metaphor, Nation, and the Holocaust: The Concept of the Body Politic*. London: Routledge.

Mussolini, Benito (1925) 'Celebrazione della vittoria', in *Omnia Opera di Benito Mussolini*. Florence, La Fenice, Vol. 29, pp. 439–41.

Mussolini, Benito (1933) *The Political and Social Doctrine of Fascism*. London: Hogarth Press; orig. pubd in *Enciclopedia Italiana* of 1932 under the heading 'Fascismo'.

Nagle, John (1970) *The National Democratic Party: Right Radicalism in the Federal Republic of Germany*. Berkeley: University of California Press.

Nelis, Jan (2007) 'Constructing Fascist identity: Benito Mussolini and the myth of Romanità', *Classical World*, 100(4): 391–415.

Nelis, Jan, Morelli, Anne and Praet, Danny (eds) (2015) *Catholicism and Fascism in Europe 1918–1945*. Hildesheim: Georg Olms.

Neocleous, Mark (1997) *Fascism*. Minneapolis: University of Minnesota Press.

Neumann, Franz (1942) *Behemoth: The Structure and Practice of National Socialism*. London: Victor Gollancz.

Neumann, Klaus (2017) 'Interwar Germany and the corporatist wave, 1918–1939', in António Costa Pinto (ed.), *Corporatism and Fascism: The Corporatist Wave in Europe*. London: Routledge.

Niven, William (2000) 'The birth of Nazi drama? *Thing* plays', in John London (ed.), *Theatre Under the Nazis*. Manchester: Manchester University Press, pp. 54–95.

Nociar, Tomáš (2017) 'The Kotleba phenomenon', *Hate Speech International*, 3 January, www.hate-speech.org/kotleba-phenomenon/.

Nolte, Ernst (1965) *Three Faces of Fascism: Action Française,*

Italian Fascism, National Socialism. New York: Holt, Rinehart & Winston.

O'Meara, Michael (2013) *New Culture, New Right: Anti-Liberalism in Postmodern Europe.* London: Arktos.

Ohana, David (1991) 'Georges Sorel and the rise of political myth', *History of European Ideas,* 13(6): 733–46.

Ortega y Gasset, José (1932) *The Revolt of the Masses.* London: W. W. Norton.

Osborne, Peter (1995) *The Politics of Time: Modernity and the Avant-Garde.* London: Verso.

Outhwaite, William (1983) *Concept Formation in Social Science.* London: Routledge & Kegan Paul.

Outhwaite, William (ed.) (2002) *The Blackwell Dictionary of Modern Social Thought.* Oxford: Blackwell.

Overy, Stephen (2001) 'Gramsci and the German crisis, 1929–34: A historical interpretation of the Prison Notebooks', PhD dissertation, University of York.

Ozouf, Mona (1989) *L'homme régénéré: essais sur la révolution.* Paris: Gallimard.

Pager, Tyler (2016) 'Gary Johnson: Trump is a fascist', *Politico,* 23 August, www.politico.com/story/2016/08/gary-johnson-trump-fascist-227339#ixzz4LRuPKpSO.

Parsons, Talcott (1954) 'Some sociological aspects of fascist movements', *Essays in Sociological Theory.* Glencoe, IL: Free Press, pp. 124–41.

Passmore, Kevin (2002) *Fascism: A Very Short Introduction.* Oxford: Oxford University Press.

Passmore, Kevin (ed.) (2003) *Women, Gender, and Fascism in Europe, 1919–45.* Manchester: Manchester University Press.

Paxton, Robert (2004) *The Anatomy of Fascism.* New York: Knopf Doubleday.

Payne, Geoffrey (2006) 'Methodological pluralism', in Victor Jupp (ed.), *The Sage Dictionary of Social Research Methods.* London: Sage, pp. 174–6.

Payne, Stanley G. (1961) *Falange: A History of Spanish Fascism.* Stanford, CA: Stanford University Press.

Payne, Stanley G. (1980a) 'The concept of fascism', in Stein Larsen, Bernt Hagtvet and Jan Petter Myklebust (eds), *Who Were the Fascists? Social Roots of European Fascism.* Oslo: Universitetsforlaget, pp. 14–25.

Payne, Stanley G. (1980b) *Fascism: Comparison and Definition.* Madison: University of Wisconsin Press.

Payne, Stanley G. (1995) *A History of Fascism, 1914–1945.* London: UCL Press.

Pearce, William ([1978] 2013) *The Turner Diaries*. Raleigh, NC: Lulu Press.

Pellicani, Luciano (2003) *Revolutionary Apocalypse: Ideological Roots of Terrorism*. Santa Barbara, CA: Praeger.

Pellicani, Luciano (2012) 'Fascism, capitalism, modernity', *European Journal of Political Theory*, 11(4): 394–409.

Petersen, Julius (1934) *Die Sehnsucht nach dem Dritten Reich in deutscher Sage und Dichtung*. Stuttgart: Metzler.

Pine, Lisa (1997) *Nazi Family Policy, 1933–1945*. London: Bloomsbury.

Pine, Lisa (2007) *Hitler's National Community*. London: Bloomsbury.

Platon, Mircea (2012) 'The Iron Guard and the "modern state": Iron Guard leaders Vasile Marin and Ion I. Moța, and the "New European Order"', *Fascism*, 1(2): 65–90.

Platt, Gerald (1980) 'Thoughts on a theory of collective action: Language, affect and ideology in revolution', in Mel Albin (ed.), *New Directions in Psychohistory: The Adelphi Papers in Honor of Erik H. Erikson*. Lexington, MA: Lexington Books, pp. 69–94.

Pohlmann, Friedrich (2008) 'Bolschewismus und Nationalsozialismus: Ideologie, Herrschaftsstrukturen und Terrorsysteme der totalitären Antipoden', *Totalitarismus und Demokratie*, 5(2): 163–203.

Pois, Robert (1986) *National Socialism and the Religion of Nature*. New York: St Martin's Press.

Poliakov, Léon (1974) *The Aryan Myth: A History of Racist and Nationalist Ideas in Europe*. New York: Basic Books.

Ponchaud, François (1978) *Cambodia: Year Zero*. New York: Holt, Rinehart & Winston.

Ponzio, Alessio (2017) *Shaping the New Man: Youth Training Regimes in Fascist Italy and Nazi Germany*. Madison: University of Wisconsin Press.

Popper, Karl ([1957] 2002) *The Poverty of Historicism*. London: Kegan Paul.

Poulantzas, Nicos (1979) *Fascism and Dictatorship*. London: Verso.

Pound, Ezra (1935) *Make it New*. New Haven, CT: Yale University Press.

Quartermaine, Luisa (2000) *Mussolini's Last Republic: Propaganda and Politics in the Italian Social Republic (R.S.I.) 1943–45*. Chicago: Intellect Books.

Quine, Maria Sophia (2002) *Italy's Social Revolution: Charity and Welfare from Liberalism to Fascism*. Basingstoke: Palgrave Macmillan.

Quine, Maria Sophia (2012) 'Racial "sterility" and "hyperfecundity" in Fascist Italy: Biological politics of sex and reproduction', *Fascism*, 1(2): 92–144.

Rauschning, Hermann (1939) *The Revolution of Nihilism: Warning to the West*. New York: Longmans, Green.

Rauschning, Hermann (1940) *The Voice of Destruction*. New York: G. P. Putnam's Sons.

Reich, Wilhelm ([1933] 1936) *The Mass Psychology of Fascism*. New York: Orgone Institute.

Reichardt, Sven (2009) *Faschistische Kampfbünde: Gewalt und Gemeinschaft im italienischen Squadrismus und in der deutschen SA*. Cologne: Böhlau.

Renton, David (1999) *Fascism: Theory and Practice*. London: Pluto Press.

Ricci, Steven (2008) *Cinema and Fascism: Italian Film and Society, 1922–1943*. Berkeley: University of California Press.

Riddell, John (2012) 'Introduction', in Riddell (ed.), *Toward the United Front: Proceedings of the Fourth Congress of the Communist International, 1922*. London: Haymarket Books.

Riddell, John (2014) 'Fumble and late recovery: The Comintern response to Italian Fascism', https://johnriddell.wordpress.com/2014/06/01/fumble-and-late-recovery-the-comintern-response-to-italian-fascism.

Roberts, David (2000) 'How not to think about fascism and ideology, intellectual antecedents and historical meaning', *Journal of Contemporary History*, 35(2): 185–211.

Roberts, David (2006) *The Totalitarian Experiment in Twentieth-Century Europe: Understanding the Poverty of Great Politics*. London: Routledge.

Roberts, David (2010) 'Fascism, Marxism, and the question of modern revolution', *European Journal of Political Theory*, 9(2): 183–201.

Roberts, David (2011) 'Reconsidering Gramsci's interpretation of Fascism', *Journal of Modern Italian Studies*, 16(2): 239–55.

Roberts, David (2016) *Fascist Interactions: Proposals for a New Approach to Fascism and its Era*. New York: Berghahn Books.

Roberts, David and Griffin, Roger (2012) *European Journal of Political Theory*, 11(4) [special issue: *The 'Fascist Revolution': Utopia or Façade? Reconciling Marxist and Non-Marxist Approaches*].

Roberts, Hanna (2012) 'The Ku Klux Klan unmasked: Extraordinary images from a divisive era capture a day of reckoning when 50,000 white supremacists marched on Capitol Hill', *Mail Online*, 12 February, www.dailymail.co.uk/news/article-2100077/Ku-Klux-Klan-Extraordinary-images-divisive-era-capture-day-reckoning-50-000-white-supremacists-marched-Washington-DC. html.

Robins-Early, Nick (2015) 'A field guide to Europe's radical right political parties', *Huffington Post*, 12 February.

Robinson, R. A. H. (1981) *Fascism in Europe*. London: Historical Association.

Rohkrämer, Thomas (2007) *A Single Communal Faith? The German Right from Conservatism to National Socialism*. New York: Berghahn Books.

Ross, Alexander (2017) *Against the Fascist Creep*. Chico, CA: AK Press.

Rusu, Mihai (2016) 'The sacralization of martyric death in Romanian Legionary Movement: Self-sacrificial patriotism, vicarious atonement, and thanatic nationalism', *Politics, Religion & Ideology*, 17(2–3): 249–73.

Saba, Paul (ed.) (1979) 'The concept of "social-fascism" and the relationship between social-democracy and fascism', chapter 9 in Bay Area Study Group, *On the Roots of Revisionism: A Political Analysis of the International Communist Movement and the CPUSA, 1919–1945*, www.marxists.org/history/erol/1946-1956/roots-revisionism/index.htm.

Salvatorelli, Luigi ([1924] 1977) *Nazionalfascismo*. Turin: Einaudi.

Sandulescu, Valentin (2004) 'Fascism and its quest for the "New Man": The case of the Romanian Legionary Movement', *Studia Hebraica*, no. 4: 349–61.

Santoro, Lorenzo (2012) 'Antonio Gramsci: The fascist leadership as modern reactionary Caesarism and the novelty of the corporative state', *Leadership*, 8(6): 277–86.

Schieder, Wolfgang (2008) *Faschistische Diktaturen: Studien zu Italien und Deutschland*. Göttingen: Wallstein.

Schnapp, Jeffrey (2004) 'Rayon/Marinetti', in Pierpaolo Antonello and Simon Gilson (eds), *Science and Literature in Italian Culture from Dante to Calvino*. Oxford: Legenda: 226–53.

Schoenbaum, David (1966) *Hitler's Social Revolution: Class and Status in Nazi Germany 1933–1939*. New York: Doubleday.

Scruton, Roger (1983) *A Dictionary of Political Thought*. London: Pan Books.

Seierstad, Åsne (2015) *One of Us: The Story of a Massacre and its Aftermath*. London: Virago.

Shapira, Avraham (1996) 'Individual self and national self in the thought of Aaron David Gordon', *Jewish Studies Quarterly*, 3(3): 280–99.

Sheinin, David and Baer Barr, Lois (eds) (1996) *The Jewish Diaspora in Latin America: New Studies on History and Literature.* New York: Garland.

Shekhovtsov, Anton (2008a) 'By cross and sword: "Clerical fascism" in interwar Western Ukraine', in Matthew Feldman and Marius Turda (eds), *Clerical Fascism in Interwar Europe.* London: Routledge, pp. 59–73.

Shekhovtsov, Anton (2008b) 'The palingenetic thrust of Russian neo-Eurasianism: Ideas of rebirth in Aleksandr Dugin's worldview', *Totalitarian Movements and Political Religions,* 9(4): 491–506.

Shekhovtsov, Anton (2012) 'European far-right music and its enemies', in Ruth Wodak and John Richardson (eds), *Analyzing Fascist Discourse: European Fascism in Talk and Text.* London: Routledge, pp. 277–96.

Shekhovtsov, Anton (2015) 'Russian politicians building an international extreme right alliance', *Anton Shekhovtsov's Blog,* 15 September, http://anton-shekhovtsov.blogspot.co.uk/2015/09/russian-politicians-building.html.

Shekhovtsov, Anton (2016) 'The Ukrainian far right and the Ukrainian Revolution', in *New Europe College Black Sea Link Program Yearbook 2014–2015.* Romania: New Europe College, pp. 215–37.

Shekhovtsov, Anton (2017) *Russia and the Western Far Right.* London: Routledge.

Shenfield, Stephen (2001) *Russian Fascism: Traditions, Tendencies, Movements.* Armonk, NY: M. E. Sharpe.

Soucy, Robert (1979) *Fascist Intellectual: Drieu la Rochelle.* Berkeley: University of California Press.

Soucy, Robert (1986) *French Fascism: The First Wave, 1924–1933.* New Haven, CT: Yale University Press.

Stephenson, Jill (2001) *Women in Nazi Germany.* London: Routledge.

Sternhell, Zeev (1976) 'Fascist ideology', in Walter Laqueur (ed.), *Fascism: A Reader's Guide.* Berkeley: University of California Press, pp. 315–76.

Sternhell, Zeev (1986) *Neither Right, nor Left: Fascist Ideology in France.* Berkeley: University of California Press.

Sternhell, Zeev (1987) 'Fascism', in David Miller (ed.), *The Blackwell Encyclopedia of Political Thought.* Oxford: Blackwell.

Sternhell, Zeev (2010) *The Anti-Enlightenment Tradition.* New Haven, CT: Yale University Press.

Stone, Maria (1998) *The Patron State: Culture and Politics in Fascist Italy.* Princeton, NJ: Princeton University Press.

Streel, José ([1942] 2010) *La révolution du XXème siècle,* ed. Lionel Baland. Paris: Déterna.

Sunic, Thomas (2012) *Against Democracy and Equality: The European New Right*. London: Arktos.

Szabados, Krisztian (2015) 'The particularities and uniqueness of Hungary's Jobbik', in Giorgos Charalambous (ed.), *The European Far Right: Historical and Contemporary Perspectives*. Nicosia: PRIO Cyprus, pp. 49–57.

Szele, Aron (2015) *The Arrow Cross: The Ideology of Hungarian Fascism: A Conceptual Approach*. Budapest: Central European University, http://archive.ceu.hu/node/23962 [PhD thesis].

Tansman, Ian (ed.) (2009) *The Culture of Japanese Fascism*. Durham, NC: Duke University Press.

Theweleit, Klaus (1987, 1991) *Male Fantasies*, 2 vols. Minneapolis: University of Minnesota Press.

Thies, Jochen (2012) *Hitler's Plans for Global Domination: Nazi Architecture and Ultimate War Aims*. New York: Berghahn Books.

Thomson, Alexander Raven (1935) *The Coming Corporate State*. London: Action Press.

Thurlow, Richard (1987) *Fascism in Britain: A History 1918–85*. Oxford: Oxford University Press.

Tilles, Daniel (2014) *British Fascist Antisemitism and Jewish Responses, 1932–40*. London: Bloomsbury.

Tomasevich, Jozo (2001) *War and Revolution in Yugoslavia, 1941–1945: Occupation and Collaboration*. Stanford, CA: Stanford University Press.

Tooze, Adam (2006) *The Wages of Destruction: The Making and Breaking of the Nazi Economy*. London: Allen Lane.

Trajano Filho, Francisco (2017) 'The many faces of the same body: Architecture, politics and power in Vargas' regime (1930–1945)', *Fascism*, 6(2) [special issue on Latin architecture in the era of fascism].

Trotsky, Leon (1933) 'What is National Socialism?', *Modern Thinker*, October; www.marxists.org/archive/trotsky/germany/1933/330610.htm.

Trotsky, Leon (1934) 'Bonapartism and Fascism', *New International*, 1(2): 37–8; www.marxists.org/archive/trotsky/germany/1934/340715.htm.

Turda, Marius (2008a) 'Conservative palingenesis and cultural modernism in early twentieth-century Romania', *Totalitarian Movements and Political Religions*, 9(4): 437–53.

Turda, Marius (2008b) 'National historiographies in the Balkans, 1830–1989', in Stefan Berger and Chris Lorenz (eds), *The Contested Nation: Ethnicity, Class, Religion and Gender in*

National Histories. Basingstoke: Palgrave Macmillan, pp. 463–89.

Turda, Marius (2010) *Modernism and Eugenics*. Basingstoke: Palgrave Macmillan.

Turda, Marius (ed.) (2015) 'Romania', in *The History of East-Central European Eugenics, 1900–1945: Sources and Commentaries*. London: Bloomsbury, pp. 271–361.

Turda, Marius and Gillette, Aaron (2014) *Latin Eugenics in Comparative Perspective*. London: Bloomsbury.

Turner, Henry A. (1975) 'Fascism and modernization', in *Reappraisals of Fascism*. New York: New Viewpoints.

Turner, Henry A. (ed.) (1985) *German Big Business and the Rise of Hitler*. Oxford: Oxford University Press.

Umland, Andreas (2010) 'Aleksandr Dugin's transformation from a lunatic fringe figure into a mainstream political publicist, 1980–1998: A case study in the rise of late and post-Soviet Russian fascism', *Journal of Eurasian Studies*, 1(2): 144–52.

Umland, Andreas (2015) 'Challenges and promises of comparative research into post-Soviet fascism: Methodological and conceptual issues in the study of the contemporary East European extreme right', *Communist and Post-Communist Studies*, 48(2–3): 169–81.

UNESCO (1969) *Four Statements on the Race Question*. Paris: UNESCO.

Vajda, Mihaly (1976) *Fascism as a Mass Movement*. New York: St Martin's Press.

Vasilopoulou, Sofia and Halikiopoulou, Daphne (2015) *The Golden Dawn's 'Nationalist Solution': Explaining the Rise of the Far Right in Greece*. Basingstoke: Palgrave Macmillan.

Verkhovsky, Alexander (ed.) (2016) *The Ultra-Right Movement under Pressure: Xenophobia and Radical Nationalism in Russia, and Efforts to Counteract Them in 2015*. Moscow: SOVA Center Reports, www.sova-center.ru/en/xenophobia/reports-analyses/2016/04/d34247/.

von Beckerath, Erwin (1927) *Wesen und Werden des faschistischen Staates*. Berlin: Springer.

Vondung, Klaus (1971) *Magie und Manipulation: Ideologischer Kult und politische Religion des Nationalsozialismus*. Göttingen: Vandenhoeck & Ruprecht.

Wahnón, Sultana (2017) 'The architectural myth of Spanish fascism: A new architecture for a new empire', *Fascism*, 6(2) [special issue on Latin architecture in the era of fascism].

Weber, Eugen (1964) *Varieties of Fascism: Doctrines of Revolution in the Twentieth Century*. New York: Van Nostrand.

Weber, Max ([1904] 1949) 'Objectivity in social science and social policy', in Edward A. Shils and Henry A. Finch (ed. and trans.), *The Methodology of the Social Sciences*. New York: Free Press.

Weiss-Wendt, Anton and Yeomans, Rory (eds) (2013) *Racial Science in Hitler's New Europe, 1938–1945*. Lincoln: University of Nebraska Press.

Whittam, John (1995) *Fascist Italy*. Manchester: Manchester University Press.

Wippermann, Wolfgang (2009) *Faschismus: Eine Weltgeschichte vom 19. Jahrhundert bis heute*. Darmstadt: Primus.

Woodley, Daniel (2009) *Fascism and Political Theory: Critical Perspectives on Fascist Ideology*. London: Routledge.

Woolf, Stuart (1968) *The Nature of Fascism*. London: Weidenfeld & Nicolson [proceedings of a conference held by the Reading University Graduate School of Contemporary European Studies].

Yahya, Harun (2002) *Fascism: The Bloody Ideology of Darwinism*, http://harunyahya.com/en/Books/658/Fascism-The-Bloody-Ideology-of-Darwinism.

Yannielli, Joseph (2012) 'The nationalist international: Or what American history can teach us about the fascist revolution', *European Journal of Political Theory*, 11(4): 438–58.

Yeomans, Rory (2002) 'Fighting the white plague: Demography and abortion in the independent state of Croatia', in Christian Promitzer, Sevastē Troumpeta and Marius Turda (eds), *Health, Hygiene, and Eugenics in Southeastern Europe to 1945*. Pittsburgh: Pittsburgh University Press.

Yeomans, Rory (2013) *Visions of Annihilation: The Ustasha Regime and the Cultural Politics of Fascism, 1941–1945*. Pittsburgh: University of Pittsburgh Press.

Yockey, Francis ([1948] 1962) *Imperium: The Philosophy of History and Politics*. Washington, DC: Legion for the Survival of Freedom.

Yockey, Francis ([1949] 2012) *The Proclamation of London of the European Liberation Front*. Shamley Green, Surrey: Palingenesis Project.

Zunino, Pier-Giorgio (1985) *L'ideologia del fascismo*. Bologna: Il Mulino.

Index